Diary of a Lonely Prom Queen

Reflections on Parenting
Teenage Girls
From a Teenage Survivor

D1373855

Tabitha Eichelberger

outskirts
press

Diary of a Lonely Prom Queen
Reflections on Parenting Teenage Girls from a Teenage Survivor
All Rights Reserved.
Copyright © 2018 Tabitha Eichelberger
v2.0

The opinions expressed in this manuscript are solely the opinions of the author and do not represent the opinions or thoughts of the publisher. The author has represented and warranted full ownership and/or legal right to publish all the materials in this book.

This book may not be reproduced, transmitted, or stored in whole or in part by any means, including graphic, electronic, or mechanical without the express written consent of the publisher except in the case of brief quotations embodied in critical articles and reviews.

Outskirts Press, Inc.
http://www.outskirtspress.com

ISBN: 978-1-9772-0123-2

Library of Congress Control Number: 2018907971

Cover Image by Tabitha Eichelberger

Outskirts Press and the "OP" logo are trademarks belonging to Outskirts Press, Inc.

PRINTED IN THE UNITED STATES OF AMERICA

Table of Contents

Dedication

I want to dedicate this book to one of my biggest inspirations, my daughter, Tinley. You consistently amaze me with your caring and soft-hearted spirit. Your laughter is contagious, your innocence is priceless, and your genuine love for people is inspiring. As you grow up and life happens, my wish for you is that you never change who you are. You are beautifully and wonderfully made! You will always be my princess, Tinley Sue and I love you more than you'll ever know!

Author's Notes

- **** = Words spoken from my mother*

- *Some names and likenesses have been changed for anonymity purposes.*

Introduction

WE'VE ALL BEEN there, the high school homecoming dance. A teacher leans into the mic and orders everyone to be quiet as he or she announces the homecoming court for that year. Some people roll their eyes, others ignore what's going on completely, and others wish more than anything that they could be the ones walking down that aisle.

I was part of the latter group. I was a freshman at my first homecoming, and all the students had lined up to wait for the introduction of the court. This single moment remains vivid in my mind. As I heard the king and queen announced and watched them walk down the aisle, I thought to myself, "I want to be that girl." The queen had it all. She was beautiful and outgoing, had lots of friends, was full of confidence, and— perhaps most importantly—everyone loved her.

And so a new goal was born: I would become the queen someday. I knew that if I could be the queen, things would be good in my world. Being the queen meant I would have the friends I wanted, the social acceptance I needed, and the popularity so many of us strived for.

Four years later my dream came true. I walked down that same aisle as Paxton-Buckley-Loda High School's 2003 homecoming queen. What were once just fantasies inscribed on the pages of my journal, were now a reality.

However, what I had dreamt would be this magically perfect moment somehow didn't fit my reality. I didn't have the feelings I had expected. I didn't have the friends I thought I would. I didn't feel accepted. Walking down that aisle stirred some sort of strange nostalgia inside me. Four years earlier, I had thought this would be all I needed to make me happy. And to be honest, at that very moment I really was happy, but not for the reasons I had expected.

I was grateful that I had been chosen to receive this award, which in my mind meant that some of my peers obviously had to like me, yet I was confused as I looked around at my peers cheering, clapping, and congratulating me. I remember thinking to myself, "How could I have possibly won this when none of the people cheering for me are my true friends? None of them invite me to sit with them at lunch or go out with them on the weekends. How can all these people like me if they really don't know me at all? Why do I feel so lonely and out of place all the time?"

On the outside I was waving to my peers, smiling from ear to ear as the photographer snapped pictures, laughing with the king as the music began to play. But on the inside, I was just a lonely girl, looking around desperately for someone to call my friend. Interesting how so many times outward appearances are the most deceiving.

PART 1
MY JOURNEY

CHAPTER 1

The Stereotype

OKAY, PARENTS, TAKE your mind back to your teenage years and think about the first thing that comes to mind when you hear the following: *Cheerleader. Homecoming Queen. Prom Queen. Dating the class president.*

I'm guessing your thoughts are probably similar to what mine were before I went into high school. *Popular? Super social? Overconfident? Outgoing? Snobby? Mean girl?* Any of these thoughts pop into your mind?

I was a cheerleader from my sophomore to senior year. I was elected prom princess my junior year, and was both the homecoming queen and prom queen my senior year. My longtime boyfriend was an outgoing, funny and charismatic class president who seemed to get along with everyone. I had a wonderful home life with two loving parents and little sister. What more could a girl ask for, right?

When doing research for this book, I decided to ask some of my former classmates to tell me what type of person they saw me as in high school. I knew I was taking a risk as I asked people from all different social groups, including some who I didn't think liked me too well. My goal was to find out people's real notions of who I was at that time.

The responses I got were mixed. Some classmates—interestingly enough, ALL of my male classmates—were very willing to share their perceptions and got back to me right away. However, most of the women I asked either did not respond or seemed to have a reason as to why they weren't able to answer my questions. Of the responses I did receive, here are some of them:

Q. Describe the type of person you saw me as in school.
A. Beautiful, intelligent, nice, compassionate, friendly, outgoing, well-mannered

Okay, got those thoughts in your mind? Now clear your mind. I want you to tell me what type of person you think of when you hear this description: anxious, on medication for depression since the age of sixteen, misfit, lonely, sad, suffers from suicidal thoughts and tendencies. Okay, got it? What do you think? Are there people you know who would fit either description? Would it be strange to think that one person would fit both descriptions? Well, this was me—hiding behind a smile, and exuding a confident, happy demeanor on the outside while consistently battling the pain and loneliness I felt inside. I did this every day, all day, for the majority of my teenage years.

Seems a bit contradictory, right? These two types of people don't mix. It doesn't make sense. How can a person seem so happy, so well liked and successful, yet be absolutely miserable and hate life at the same time?

I know I can't be the only teenage or for that matter, the only woman who has gone through this. As a matter of fact, in researching for this book, I found that almost every woman I talked to about her teenage years expressed some of the same feelings I had.

So, parents, instead of brushing these anxieties under the rug and trying to forget some of the ugliness of our own past, let's take off our masks, let our guard down, and sift through some of the dirt and grime that some of us may have stuffed away for years. It's when we get real with ourselves and our issues that we can begin to help not only ourselves, but also our children, who may be dealing with some of the same hurt and pain that we went through as teens—and may still be going through even as adults.

CHAPTER 2

The Queen and Her Royal Family (Girl World)

The Royal Family

IN ORDER TO understand the world of girls I think it's easiest to break it down into levels. In many ways, their world reminds me a lot of a royal court. In any school I've ever attended or visited, I see the same thing: very defined groups, usually made up of about eight to ten girls.

There are usually two or three that form the inner circle/royal family. (Yes, they usually congregate in a circular formation—literally!) These girls make up what I call the queen and her princesses.

Surrounding them are three or four girls in the outer circle. I like to call them members of the royal court.

You then have a couple of stragglers at the edge of the circle, sometimes not even technically in the circle. These are lower court members.

Then, of course, you have the rest of the school. For lack of a better word, I'll call them commoners or peasants.

The queen is obviously the leader. She is usually very outgoing, appears confident and happy, and is usually very attractive. She's involved in a lot of activities and always seems to have a smile on her face. Parents, I'm sure all of you can look back to your teen years and remember who the queen was in your class. I sure do. For the sake of simplicity in this book, let's call her Kaci.

Kaci would walk into a room, and things would seem to hit slow motion, just like in the movies. She would walk with a slight jump in her step, and one arm would swing back and forth while the other would hold her books. She seemed to always be smiling or laughing. Her laugh alone would completely command a room, not because it was loud or obnoxious, but because her presence possessed a certain aura. There was almost a glow to it. Obviously, I'm not being literal here, but can you picture what I'm getting at?

Kaci was good at sports, had a beautiful voice and looked like she belonged on the cover of a magazine. She was also one of the first girls in our class to date an upperclassman. She was definitely the envy of many in our class, but she wasn't the "mean girl" some might imagine.

Surprisingly, many times the queen isn't the mean one. Queens obviously have some confidence, or they wouldn't be in the position they are in. However, because of this confidence, they don't necessarily feel the need to be mean to others.

Can they be mean? Of course! But it's usually the princesses you have to watch out for.

Many times, princesses are the queen's best friends—or so the queen may think. Most of the princesses I have encountered are not really friends at all. They are, however, stellar actresses. They are the queen's closest confidants. They are at her every beck and call. They laugh when she laughs, sit when she sits, eat when she eats; they're pretty much human shadows. Just by observing them, you would think the queen has an unbreakable bond with her princesses; however, if you watch for long enough, you will begin to see their inner vultures come out.

Ever so patiently, these princesses will circle and wait. They wait for the queen to make the slightest misstep. As soon as she trips up, they turn on her in an instant and try to take her crown. This situation could arise from something as simple as the queen getting sick and missing school for a few days. The court needs someone to follow. (I mean, how could they function without a leader?) A princess will step up to the position without missing a beat. She may appear distraught that her beloved queen isn't feeling well and makes sure everyone knows just how concerned she is about the queen's well-being. The princess, however, makes sure to be just a little nicer than the queen and dress a little more noticeably than the queen. And somehow during the queen's absence secrets that are only known by a select few are suddenly leaked to the court. (You guessed it—the princesses know what to do.) Of course, this is not done maliciously in any way; it is more out of concern for the queen's well-being. Right?

It might just happen to get out that the queen messed around with the boyfriend of a lower court member the weekend before. Or it's leaked that the queen mentioned that the only reason "Jane" made the volleyball team was because Jane's dad, a very prominent figure in town, seemed to be let's say "influencing" the coach's decisions. Perhaps he was inviting her to upscale social events, affording her opportunities that seemed a bit out of her league? These types of leaks are usually what will ultimately lead to the queen's demise. It doesn't take much before there is a new queen in town.

The Court

Court members play a big role in the royal family's success or failure. If the court weren't there, there wouldn't be a royal family at all. They are the ones who allow the queen to be in control. They look up to the queen and do whatever they need to stay in her—and the family's—good graces. Their ambition is toward upward mobility. Many times, this is done by living a lifestyle that the royals endorse, whether that be surrounding themselves with people close to the family, behaving in ways the family commends, or even dressing and talking the way the family does. They fight and scratch their way to the top and continue fighting once they get there, pushing people down in the process.

I'm visualizing a ropes course in my mind. It's a race to see who can make it to the top first. I see members of the court pushing others down and watching them fall aimlessly to the ground as they make their way to the top. Once they finally reach the top, however, their work isn't finished. It's just beginning. They are constantly in a battle to fight off others in order to keep their position in the court. Members of the court are always on guard, and just like the princesses, they are constantly waiting for a royal to make a mistake so that they can climb up just a little higher on the social ladder.

Unfortunately, most court members don't have much self-esteem at all. They have conformed extensively and given up much of who they are in order to be what they think the court wants them to be. They don't recognize or value the people they were in the first place. Members of the court are always thinking about how to increase their positions in society—many times at the expense of others.

Lower Court

While lower court members may have a friend in the court or know a member of the royal family, they aren't really closely entwined with the royals or the lifestyle.

Lower court members may dream about being a part of the court, but they also know they don't have the necessary means to ever really become one of them. In Girl World, this could be because they don't have the finances to wear the name brand clothes, or they may not be very good at sports, or they may just not have the type of personality that attracts people to them. In the world of girls, however, things just seem to work in a way that excludes people who don't conform to a certain style.

Commoners

This category is where most people fit. In royal societies, and really societies in general, only a select few are members of the elite. Most of the population consists of regular people trying to live a good life.

Commoners, unlike lower court members, aren't really involved with the royals at all. It doesn't mean they are not special or good people. Actually, as a teenager, the few true friends I had were in this category and were much better friends to me than any court member ever was. These girls are usually quite fun and interesting in part because they aren't so obsessed with trying to fit in and are more comfortable letting their real personality be known to those around them. They may be aware of who the royals are or hear something about them at one time or another, but they don't really care much about what goes on in the royal family. They see the royals as untouchables, occupying a celebrity-like status.

Commoners know they are not going to be part of the royal family and are okay with the fact that they will probably never become one of them. Commoners have their own groups of friends, their own problems and issues, and basically don't care much about what goes on in the family. Although the title "commoner" isn't the most appealing, in many ways I always thought being a commoner would be much easier and less pretentious than being a royal.

Commoners don't have to worry about keeping up a façade and constantly fighting off others for a position. They know they are not ever going to be a royal, and therefore don't feel the pressure to inch their way up the ladder. They accept their position in society and often focus their lives on more meaningful and important tasks.

In Girl World, this could mean focusing on their education more than socializing, or they could have more meaningful, deep friendships because they are able to be themselves instead of putting up a façade in order to keep the positions they are in.

As one of the few who transitioned from commoner to queen and then to somewhere in the middle, I was more of an exception to the rule. I would take being a commoner any day over the pressure of being the queen or a member of her royal court. Commoners are actually pretty awesome if you ask me!

CHAPTER 3

Lines

IT'S INTERESTING HOW you can tell so easily in any school, who the queen is, who the princesses are, and who is in the queen's court just by looking at something as simple as the line up in a sporting event.

In 8th grade volleyball, we would always line up before the games and run out onto the court together to do our warm-ups. No matter how much I wanted to be first or second in line, it was always the queen first, followed by two or three princesses, and then trailed by the rest of the court. Then there was me and maybe—if I was lucky— one or two behind me.

We would do the typical volleyball warm-up—throw, bump, set, spike—over and over again. While doing this, I remember trying to think rationally to myself, "How is it that these girls all seem to fight so hard for this first spot when, in reality, who cares if they are first in line or last?"

Well, the truth was that I cared. And they cared. In fact, everyone on that team cared where they were in the lineup. The funny thing was that the lineup had nothing to do with volleyball or how good a player you were. Instead, it had everything to do with how we all wanted people to perceive us. No one wanted to be in the back of the line because that meant you weren't significant. You weren't part of the court. You weren't "one of them." I didn't necessarily want to be that first girl out on the court, or even the second or third girl. I just didn't want to always be the last.

Looking back, it's still one of my most defining memories. I remember feeling "put in my place" at the beginning of every game. No words needed to be spoken. I knew exactly where I stood on the social ladder every time we lined up.

It was the same outside of sports, too—let's take the lunch table, for example. The table setting was pre-determined long before the lunch hour came around. The queen and her princesses were always at the head of the table. Most of the time, members of the court would fight to sit closest to the queen. Then the rest of the court and "commoners" (sticking to our fairytale theme) would sit at the end of the table.

There were a few times that a couple members of the court would get to the table before the queen and her princesses. They would sit closer to the head, hoping that the queen might sit by them. This never really worked, though. In fact, I remember a couple times when the queen would move to a totally different table, very clearly sending the message without a single word that a particular member of the court was not worthy enough to sit by her.

Thinking about it now, it's funny, because I knew the whole time exactly what was going on. I couldn't understand why these girls were willing to humiliate themselves (which is really what they were doing) just to get a seat at a lunch table. Usually I was at the end of the queen's table, not because I really cared to be at that particular table—in fact, I would have felt more comfortable being at an entirely different table altogether—but because this was where my "friends" were sitting and I didn't want to sit alone. As an 8th grader (during my first year in public school since the 2nd grade), I didn't know too many people. The girls I did know were mostly lower members of the court or commoners, so I clung to them, hoping to find a friend somewhere in that mix. I tried a couple times to sit with other groups, but like the royal court, they never really seemed to let me in either.

Basically, the hierarchy is the same no matter what group you're in. Whether it's the jocks or the band geeks, the preps or the nerds--in almost every group, people are scared to death to let someone new enter because they're so afraid that they will be left out.

CHAPTER 4

Understanding Me

*** From the time you were little, you were much more content to play in your room for hours by yourself instead of having friends over to play; you really didn't care to be around other people except those you were really close to. You enjoyed your time alone and the safety of it. You were also very fearful as a child and did not like change. You did not like being away from what you were familiar with, and you would allow your imagination to run wild with fearful thoughts when you were at school or had to walk to or from school. I also think you struggled with some type of learning disorder. The school never really took the time to look into it and you learned over the years to overcome it, but school was very hard for you. It didn't come easily like it did for others. -Mom ***

One of the first memories I have of girls was in the 1ˢᵗ grade. There was a girl who had the coolest erasers. They were neon colors, and the one that sticks out the most in my mind was shaped like a green skull and cross bones. (To this day, I still don't know why I was so envious of this particular eraser!)

Trading school supplies was the trendy thing to do in the 1ˢᵗ grade in the '90s, and I would always try to trade my stuff for that eraser. She would never trade with me, no matter what I said I would give her.

One day I came to school with two new erasers that my mom had gotten me. Surely they were WAY better than her skull eraser. One of them looked like a lipstick tube and had purple, pink, and white swirls on it. The other was a half pink/half purple heart-shaped eraser that had a base it could sit on. I was so excited and made sure to let her know what I had.

She wanted them. BAD. She offered me the skull and a couple other things that I can't remember. But what I do remember about the trade was that what I wanted even more than her eraser was to be "allowed" to play with her and her friends at recess. The erasers were my bargaining tools.

I can't remember what she said, but what I do remember is how she made me feel. She was one of the princesses. Girls liked her, boys liked her, and I wanted her to like me.

We never did play together, and honestly, I can't remember if we even made the trade. What I do remember was the way I felt around her—feelings of not being good enough, of not being accepted. It felt like no matter what I did I would never be able to be one of the princesses. Looking back now, it seems so strange that even at age six I had already experienced those feelings.

*** We took you out of the public school in 3rd grade because you were falling so far behind and sent you to a private Christian school at our church. In 8th grade we decided to return you to the public school so you could have a year to transition back before high school since the private school only went through 8th grade. In a small town it is extremely difficult to be welcomed into any crowd, but it's the most difficult when adolescents are at the peak of insecurity. Your classmates were threatened to have a beautiful new girl step into the school and felt fearful of losing friends, so they were too afraid to allow you into their circle. The situation of enjoying being alone and yet having to be surrounded by hundreds of kids for 8 hours at a time, day after day, combined with your fears of being away from what you were familiar with,* *struggling so hard to learn when it came so easily for everyone else and finally not being accepted by your peers made you feel like something was wrong with you. All of these factors put together made going to school very difficult for you. ****

It was my first year back in public school after being taught in a cottage school at my church since 3rd grade. I was born and raised in a small town, where everyone knew your name, where some of your teachers were the same teachers who taught your parents, and where you knew the names of everyone in your graduating class. Even though my school was small, it was still a dramatic change to go from twelve classmates to around 120 classmates.

After practicing all summer and fall that year, I had made the 8th grade volleyball team, and I remember riding home on the bus after one of the few games my parents didn't attend. Usually I went home with my parents so I wouldn't have to sit by myself on the bus or be around the rest of the team any longer than I had to.

However, this night was different than most because there were only about four other 8th grade girls on the bus. To my surprise, they asked me to sit with them on the way home. I was shocked, but pleasantly surprised, at how nice they were to me. It was awkward at first, and I didn't know what to say to these girls who normally didn't give me the time of day, but as we started talking, things became more comfortable.

At the end of the night, the queen asked me why I didn't hang out with them more. They told me to come and sit by them the next day before school. I had always sat on the outside of the court, usually a couple bleachers in front of them. I'd listen to bits and pieces of their conversations, but they never really included me.

I graciously accepted their invitation and went home feeling ecstatic. I remember walking in from the garage to the house with my mom that night, excitedly telling her about my trip home and how I thought that this really could be the answer to our prayers. (My mom and I would pray nightly that I would be able to find a friend.) We were both so excited.

I woke up the next morning, and for the first time ever, I was looking forward to getting to school a few minutes early. Most days I would make my mom drop my sister off first and then drive around the block a couple times so I wouldn't have to sit in the gym very long before the bell rang. Today, though, was different. It was the beginning of something new—new outlooks and new friendships. Or so I hoped.

I walked into the gym and saw the court sitting in their usual spot. I went up to them and sat down next to them. I remember sitting there and thinking to myself, "Okay, this is it. They are going to start talking to me." I waited….and waited…and waited. No different than any other day.

I thought to myself, "Okay, Tab, you just need to make a little conversation to break the ice." So I said something. I can't remember what, but it must have not been too entertaining because I was met with blank stares. The court looked at me briefly and then turned around. It seemed as if they had no clue why I would think that trying to talk to them would be an acceptable thing to do. I slowly began to realize that these girls were not going to be my friends.

I began that day to understand how the system works. I started to realize there was no way in this world that these princesses were going to endanger their place in the court by letting someone new in. A couple days went by, and I kept trying, naively thinking each new day that they would remember our conversation on the bus.

Wishful thinking. Nothing changed, and I eventually stopped trying. (Looking back, I wish I had stopped trying after the first blank stare.)

Fast forward again. During my freshman year, I had a couple of friends that I'd met in 8th grade. It was obvious that they weren't going to be lifelong friends, but they provided me with someone to sit with and talk to—basic surface-level friends. During the summer prior to my freshman year, I also started talking to the boy who would later become my high school sweetheart. For the purposes of this book, we will call him Mark. (We'll get to know him later.)

Once I started dating Mark, I noticed my group of friends started to change. It wasn't because I wanted them to, but slowly I noticed my old group of friends fading into the background. They didn't seem to want to do much outside of school with me, and I began to notice them throwing little jabs at me. They would say things like, "The only reason he's dating you is for your looks" or "You shouldn't have made the cheerleading squad—you don't even know how to do a cart-wheel!" They would laugh through these comments like they were half-joking, but their words hurt and I found myself slowly begin to pull away from them, surrounding myself with Mark's group of friends more and more.

His friends were in the court, and I must admit that it was kind of a nice feeling because, for once in my life, I started to feel like I had a real group of girlfriends. We would have sleepovers on the weekends, host parties, go to events together, and for about six months, I actually loved life! It wasn't long, though, before I started to feel pressure to "keep up with the court." For some reason, it seemed like if I didn't spend every minute with these girls both inside and outside of school that I would miss out on something. I didn't think much of it at first—I have always enjoyed having time to myself and didn't see the need to be with the court all the time—however, I soon realized my lifestyle would not work in Girl World.

Before long, I could feel myself fading into the background. To this day I don't know exactly why this happened, but I was replaced in court just as quickly as I had entered. However, interestingly enough, I was still considered by most of the school to be a member of the court. Some would even say I was the "queen." Maybe it was because of who I was dating, or maybe it was because of how people stereotyped me, but in reality, I didn't have any true friends. My old friends didn't talk to me anymore. (Looking back now, I truly believe they had their own self-esteem issues and by putting me down it made them feel better about themselves). And the new friends I had started to make seemed to decide that I didn't have the "it" factor to be in their group either.

I was stuck in an awkward position. Although my classmates considered me to be very popular and well-liked because of my so-called social status, in reality I was incredibly lonely and felt out of place no matter who I surrounded myself with. After a while, I began to withdraw altogether. It became too hard to try to fit in, so I couldn't rationalize even trying. During this time, a wall started to build up around me. The compassionate heart that I had always had began to harden. I began thinking of friendships in an unhealthy way. I became possessive of my friends and tried to keep them from having other friends. If they started hanging around someone else, my mentality was: "I'll get them before they can get me." If I saw a friend starting to pull away, even if it was just a little, I would push back from that friendship and sometimes find a reason to end the friendship completely because I was so afraid that I would be eventually rejected.

I see now what I was doing was a defense mechanism, and I am sad to say that I could possibly have had more good friendships throughout my teen years if I had handled my feelings differently; however, in that moment it was easier to put up my wall than to allow myself the possibility of getting hurt again.

Although I think this hardening process started as early as 8th grade, it wasn't until my junior year that the boulders began to form. I befriended a new girl; we will call her Jade. I wrote her a note one day introducing myself and let her know that she was welcome to sit with me and my "friends" at lunch time. She was really nice, and we'd sit together in the hallway at lunch since neither of us ate school lunches in the cafeteria. After the other girls finished eating, they would come and sit with us.

At the beginning of the year, the girls in our group sat and talked to me, and Jade would listen in on the conversation. I tried to include her in our conversations and make her feel like a part. (Lord knows I knew what it felt like to be the new girl!) The change was gradual, but after a few weeks, I noticed the conversations had begun to shift. Jade started talking more with the other girls while I took more of a listening role. They started making inside jokes that I was obviously not a part of. At first, I was a little confused and unsure what to make of everything, but I tried to pretend like it was no big deal to me. One Monday we were sitting in our usual spots, and she started telling me how she went out with one of the girls the past weekend and how much fun they'd had.

What?! All of the sudden, angry thoughts started playing in my mind: "Why didn't you invite me? After all, wasn't I the one who be-friended you in the first place? I was the one who introduced you to MY friends!" Again, I tried to play it off like it was no big deal and al-luded to the fact that I had also had a super social, friend-filled party weekend. However, in reality, I spent my weekend doing my laundry, hanging out with my family, and watching movies with my boyfriend. As time went on, I gradually became the outsider, once again listen-ing in on conversations instead of being a part of them. The wall con-tinued to build boulder by boulder.

CHAPTER 5

Bullying vs. Social Isolation

IT SEEMS THE words *bully* or *bullying* are quite trendy words in today's society. It seems to be the subject matter more and more, whether on talk shows, movies, at conferences, seminars, school assemblies, etc. Bullying is a very real problem that most of us have been the victim of at some point in our lives, and while it needs to be addressed, this term is often used improperly and can be confused with another phenomenon that can be just as devastating and hurtful to a person: social isolation.

Here are the dictionary.com definitions of each:

- Bully (n): a blustering, quarrelsome, overbearing person who habitually badgers and intimidates smaller or weaker people
- Bullied, bullying (v): to be loudly arrogant and overbearing
- Social isolation (n): a state or process in which persons, groups or cultures lose or do not have communication or cooperation with one another often resulting in open conflict.

I have been privy to both types of offense; however, any bullying I experienced was short-lived, largely because of one night that still remains vivid in my mind.

In fifth grade I went to a volleyball camp through our local park district. Because I was going to a private Christian school at the time, I was beyond nervous to do this camp. I was a complete introvert back then, so I just wanted to blend in and not be noticed. I also hadn't been to public school in a couple of years and wasn't friends with anyone in the camp except one other girl who went to school with me. Needless to say, I was going in with my anxiety level high. My parents semi-made me do it because they knew it was important for me to do things outside of my comfort zone and overcome my fears.

The camp was fine. I actually can't even remember what we did during the camp sessions, but what I do remember like it was yesterday was a trip to the water fountain that rocked my world.

I stood in line quietly waiting my turn, not wanting to bring any attention to myself, when a larger, very loud girl slipped her way in front of me and pushed me further back in line. I knew what she was trying to do, and I didn't want to let her. I tried to stand still and in place so she couldn't get in front of me. When she saw my resistance, she turned and with her loud deep voice said something to the effect of "What are you going to do? You want me to punch you?"

My heart was beating a hundred miles a minute. Scared to death of getting in a fight, I put my head down and nodded "no."

She looked at me again. "Huh? I didn't think so!" she yelled.

That was it. It was all I could do to get out of line and run back to the volleyball court. A mixture of thoughts and emotions were racing through my mind. I was absolutely humiliated that someone could do that to me in front of everyone, including the one friend that I did have with me. What's more, I was scared of what the bigger girl might say to me when she saw me again—or worse yet, what she would do.

But more than anything else, I was so mad! Mad that I let her do that to me. Mad that she made me feel the way I was feeling. Mad that she thought she could push me and get away with it. Of all my feelings, this last one was the worst.

That night after I got home and had calmed down, I made a decision that has stuck with me throughout my life. I decided I never wanted to be a person who would run away again. I was not going to let someone push me around like that—physically, verbally or otherwise. I decided that I would be a person who would stand up and face my bully, even if it meant having to put up a fight. Slowly this became a motto for me: "Stand up, be noticed, and be the difference." No longer would I be the girl who ran away.

As traumatizing as that experience was for me, I was fortunate that I learned quickly how to not allow it to continue. Social isolation, on the other hand, was far worse than any type of bullying I ever experienced.

I think I can safely bet we have all been victims of social isolation at one time or another. Have you ever walked into a room only to have the conversation stop? Or have you ever sat down at a table when everyone else gets up and leaves?

Social isolation is the stereotypical "mean girl" stuff you see on TV. When you talk about girls being mean to each other or even see it happening, it may affect you a little. You might think to yourself, "Aw, that poor girl," or "Oh, I'm so glad that isn't me." But when you're the person who this is happening to, the effects can be much more devastating than people may realize.

In high school, I started sitting by myself in the hallways at lunch. I never liked school food, so I would basically wait until my "friends" got done eating, and then they would come and sit down by me. Sophomore year was the year I became part of the court. I had started seeing Mark that summer and my friends had begun to change.

At the beginning of the year, a large group would come and circle around me. I'm not going to lie and say that I didn't like all the attention I was receiving. Although it was slightly awkward to transition from being a commoner to suddenly being a high-ranking court member, I relished the idea that I was "in."

The first couple months were great, but it wasn't long before I noticed the royal court that had surrounded me was beginning to slowly move away. The more time passed, the more I noticed a new circle beginning to form. It was one that I was very obviously on the outside of. Without either group actually saying a word, I quickly realized that I was no longer welcome in their circle.

Girls know how to cut a person deeply without lifting a finger or saying a word. I racked my brain for a couple of weeks trying to think of why they weren't talking to me anymore. Had I flirted with one of their boyfriends? No. Had I said something that they could have taken offense to? I really didn't think so.

For a while I tried to join the conversation, but most of the time, I was either ignored or given the all-too-common blank stare and then ignored. I looked around at the girls that I was trying so hard to associate myself with and started to realize that we were never going to be real friends. Just by watching their interactions with the other court members, I could see clearly that they were only interested in friendships that could enhance their own status. It wouldn't have mattered if I were more genuine, fun, outgoing, or whatever else because I was not in a position to raise their social status; therefore, I didn't matter to them.

I soon decided that it wasn't worth my own time and energy to continue to invest in people who I knew didn't care about me. I also realized I was becoming exactly who I never wanted to be. I was becoming one of the girls I had always envied for their seemly confident personalities, yet at the same time I looked down upon and even pitied them a little for their chameleon-like characteristics. They consistently changed themselves in an effort to gain acceptance from the royals even if it meant making total fools of themselves in the process. I didn't want this for myself, and I didn't want others to see me this way.

I decided that instead of feeling anxious and miserable every day, waiting to see if they would accept me, I would just remove myself from the situation. Most days I would either go into a room that wasn't being used and do homework or have my mom or grandma pick me up during lunch so I didn't have to be left in that situation. Was it lonely? Absolutely! But I found it was better to be lonely by myself than to be lonely in a room full of people.

These years were hard, and I have so many more personal examples of social isolation; however, I was very blessed that God gave me a family who encouraged me from the day I was born, continuously supported me, and lifted me up in all my endeavors. From my earliest memory, my parents made sure I knew that I was of extreme value to them and to God, and this knowledge helped me build a sense of inner confidence that allowed me to get through even the darkest of times.

> ***When you were young and would go to school I put notes in your lunch box or book bag that would let you know how much you were loved, and when you got home from school I always tried to have a special snack for you. One of my favorites was making funnel cakes for you because you loved them so much. I remember giving you and your sister the "special red plate" at dinner if you had achieved something special that day, whether it be an A on a test or sometimes simply making it through the day. I wanted to make sure you knew how special and valuable you were to me.***

Even though I wanted so badly to have friends, popularity, acceptance, and so on--because of the consistent love and affirmation I received from my family I continued to gain an inner confidence and recognition of my self-worth that wouldn't allow me to become a chameleon. I couldn't allow myself to change just to be accepted by my peers, and although I did feel a certain type of pressure to be accepted, I often put more pressure on myself than others did. I think a lot of times girls talk about peer pressure and say they feel pressured to smoke, drink, have sex—the list goes on—yet I wonder if sometimes they are the ones putting pressure on themselves in the search for acceptance rather than others pressuring them?

There were times I thought about giving in to my own self-pressure simply because I was so lonely and miserable, but I knew deep down that in the long run, I would have to answer to myself and God, and I didn't want to have to say I conformed my beliefs, values, or the person God made me to be just to gain a small amount of acceptance for a short amount of time.

Unfortunately, not all children grow up in the type of loving, supportive environment that I did. In many cases, it's not because the parents don't love or care for their children. Sometimes it's just because of the way the parents were brought up. They may not know how to nurture an environment for their children that is different from the one in which they grew up. Other times it's a generational gap that confuses parents about how to interact with and understand their children, especially in today's technologically advanced society where social media is everywhere. Some parents just flat out don't know what to do!

While I am not a professional psychologist or communication expert, there are some things I have learned from my parents and other significant people in my life that I took for granted growing up. I assumed everyone already knew about these things, but as I grow older, I realize that a lot of people were not as fortunate as I and simply were not brought up with tools to know how to support and encourage their children. And if that's you, that is okay! You're reading this book to gain some knowledge and perspective about how to communicate and help your child, so you are on the right path and your intention is in the right place. You have taken a big first step, bravo to you, parent!

We must recognize that every child is different and that every child struggles with different issues, feelings and emotions and handles them in different ways. This is a good starting point toward building a foundational relationship with your child. In order to do this it's important to take inventory on our children's daily lives. Take notice of their demeanor throughout the day. When are they most happy? Sad? Talkative? Withdrawn? By figuring out their patterns and personality traits it can better help you communicate with them in the most appropriate ways. For example, I am not a morning person. I don't like to get up and talk to anyone, let alone have a meaningful conversation at 7:00 in the morning. Now wait until about 7:00 p.m. and I'm totally ready and willing to share my thoughts on the day and hear about others day.

ng up, there were two things my mom did that had a significant on me that encouraged me to want to communicate with her.

She gave me a soft place to land. There was never a time in my life when I was struggling that I couldn't go to my mom. I knew that no matter what time—day or night—she would be there to listen to me and love me. There were so many nights I remember us praying together that God would get me through the next day.

I had a college admissions advisor once tell my mom she needed to stop allowing me to share my feelings and struggles with her and that I needed to know how to handle these things myself. I thank God my mom didn't listen to him! She was my soft place. If she had even once told me to she didn't want to "hear it" or to "deal with it," it could very well have been the last straw for me. I could have done something drastic, something harmful to myself; but because I had that soft place, I didn't. I'm sure there were times she wanted to tell me to just figure it out on my own, but she knew me well enough because of the time she invested in me throughout my life. Therefore, she loved me enough to endure everything with me. She never lost hope that things would improve. For that, I will always be incredibly grateful.

> ***There was anger and frustration with the people who would cause you such pain. I knew the real Tabitha—the sweet, gentle spirit, the one whose heart broke day after day— and I wanted so badly to go to the girls and tell them what I thought of them. However, I knew this wasn't the answer; I knew this was your battle to learn to maneuver, and my job was to support and affirm you and let you know you were NEVER alone and were ALWAYS loved. Your home would ALWAYS be a safe place where you would be loved and accepted.

> Sometimes I doubted my own advice. I would share my concerns with close friends, church members, and family and ask for prayer for you. Their children all seemed so well-adjusted, and they didn't seem to struggle nearly as much as you did. It made me wonder if I was "hovering too much" and if maybe I should have just said, "toughen up and learn to deal with it,"

"this is life," "no more crying," "I'm not picking you up today, you have to stay all day," etc.

I know this parenting style may work with some kids. There are certain kids who learn to manipulate their parents, and I believe this could be the proper course for them. However, I really believed I understood you better than anyone, and you were not a manipulator. You were not "just trying to get out of school." You truly couldn't handle it and just needed help.

I have learned that although there are some great books on parenting—and I read plenty of them—EVERY child is different. It is so important to learn to understand YOUR child and his/her needs. Not all children are the same.

Another VERY important thing was that I listened, had compassion and empathy and acknowledged your feelings as genuine. At dinner time, even though you girls made fun of me, I would make you go around the table and tell us about the best thing that happened to you that day. I wanted to try to focus on the good, as well as acknowledge the bad. I thought it was important to recognize that not everything in your life was bad. We would all listen, laugh and have time together in a safe place where you felt loved and accepted***

2. My mom gave me an out. I needed to know that if things got bad enough, I could get out of the situation. I needed to know I wasn't STUCK. One of the best things my mom did was tell me that if I couldn't handle things anymore to call her and she would come get me—anytime, anyplace. She would pick me up from school for lunch about once or more a week just so I could get a break, so I didn't have to feel trapped somewhere I didn't want to be even if it was just for a few minutes. It made all the difference in the world.

My junior year, I thought I'd had as much as I could take. Mom and I prayed and prayed about what we should do, and we decided to take me out of school for an afternoon to visit a private school a few miles away. I got to see what a different school was like, and although I didn't end up changing schools, it put me at ease to know that I had that option if I needed it. Many times what made a difference wasn't the fact that I had to get out of a place, but it was knowing that I had options. That's what encouraged me and made it so much easier to stay.

*** Many days you would call from school in a panic, literally sitting in the girl's bathroom having a panic attack, and I'd tell you to just get to the lunch hour and that I would pick you up to give you a break. You would be in tears, crying that you felt like you were in prison and couldn't escape. I can remember telling you that if things ever got too bad, so bad that you thought you couldn't go on, that there were always options; things are never so bad that there isn't a way out. We would talk about options related to private schools, but I also made it clear that school itself was not an option. It is the law; you must go to school. There are some things in life that we must do, and we just have to find ways to cope and get through them and try to make the most of them; however, I never allowed you to give up or quit.

I also remember specifically reassuring you that going to school with 100+ other same-aged peers day after day for 12 years is not real life. It is the law and you must go through this to get your education, however, once you are out of school you will be surrounded by people of all ages, nationalities, beliefs, etc. When you go to work, you can walk away; you don't have to build relationships with these people. You will have relationships at work and outside of work, and you can walk in and out of the building any time you want. You can have freedom.***

CHAPTER **6**

Really, Ladies?

ALRIGHT LET'S TAKE a break from the past and fast-forward to the present. This past weekend I took four planes to four different cities. I met some very friendly folks on the plane and enjoyed getting to know a little about their lives. During the first trip, I sat next to a 20-something Indian man who was a physical therapist and another man who was a middle-aged banker from Chicago. They were both very nice, and we chatted the whole flight about everything from our careers, to family, to school, to politics. Our conversation flowed freely, and the banker even gave me his card to have me email him about some information we discussed. On the next flight, I sat with two girls who appeared to be in their mid-20s, and I believe we spoke less than ten words to each other the entire flight.

On the way home, I sat again with two more gentlemen, a hockey coach from Kansas—probably again mid-20s—and an older man from Cuba. At the beginning of the flight, I spoke with the hockey coach, mainly small talk but very pleasant. Then I started up a conversation with the Cuban man that ended up lasting over an hour. His English was broken, but we still managed to have a great deal to talk about. He told me about his country and what he did for a living and even gave me his card and told me *when* I come to Cuba to give him a call. (Perhaps I could persuade my husband to make this our next trip?!) He excitedly said he would get me the best car, hotel, and show me all around his city.

On my last flight, I sat again with a girl in her early 20s. I smiled, said "Excuse me," made one or two comments about the flight, and that is all. Can you sense a trend here? Why is it that guys are so much easier to talk to no matter what the age?

I've always had this issue. I don't consider myself a flirt—well, at least not in the past ten years!—and feel like I exhibit a pleasant demeanor toward whomever I'm with. So why is it that when I'm around women, I seem to get a stand-offish vibe from them more often than not? While reflecting on my experiences, I have come to two main conclusions about why I believe this is.

1. The Intimidation Factor

I'm just going to say it. Women are intimidated by other women. Our society has ingrained in our minds that we are not pretty enough, successful enough, smart enough, or "woman enough" in today's world.

This is no surprise; everywhere we go, there are images of the "perfect body," the "perfect woman." When you are consistently told, even if indirectly, that you are not good enough, eventually you start to believe it.

This has never been truer for me than in the past few years. For the majority of my youth, one of my main sources of confidence was my looks. I wasn't particularly smart, I wasn't the best athlete, and I really didn't have an especially outgoing personality, so my looks are what got me affirmation. I knew that I could get attention by means of my looks; I could get the affirmation I needed to feel special, no matter how wrong and warped this may sound.

Even back then, though, I still wasn't fully satisfied with how I looked. Fast forward fifteen years and two, soon-to-be three, kids later. I find myself still striving for that "perfect look." My metabolism has slowed down, hips have widened, stretch marks have appeared, and I think to myself, "I'd give anything to look like I did in high school." So what do I do? I look at others and compare myself

29

to them—everyone from the models on the cover of Vogue, to the mom sitting next to me at the preschool graduation. I can't seem to get away from it! "She has a flatter stomach than me. Her arms don't jiggle like mine." Or sometimes (and I'm not proud to admit this) I think the other way, too. "Wow, she sure has gained weight. My legs are so much better than hers."

It's absolutely awful, and I know it! I get upset when I think people are doing it to me, so why do I keep doing this to myself and others? So many of us are insecure about our own features that when we see others we think are prettier, skinnier, more successful, or whatever the case may be, we automatically get this weird inferiority complex. Whether consciously or unconsciously, we compare.

Many times, this inward feeling of inferiority displays itself outwardly, sometimes without us even realizing what we're doing. It's looking others up and down with a critical eye, it's rolling our eyes as they flip their hair or laugh loudly at a joke, or it's even the snide, slightly rude comment we make to them, just to knock them down to where we think they need to be. And why?

I don't have a textbook answer to this one. Do we think that for every eye roll we give, for every snide comment we make, we will lose a pound or our IQ will go up a point? Do we think that by being mean, we will make others somehow less attractive, smart, creative, _____ (you fill in the blank)?

In the best-case scenario, we may feel some sense of instant gratification in these moments, but even if we do, it will be very short-lived. It's not long before we begin to look at someone else and start comparing ourselves again. It becomes a consistent, unhealthy cycle and instead of trying to overcome our own self-confidence issues, we instead project our insecurities onto others to somehow try to make us feel better about ourselves.

I've been guilty of this several times, and yet as I look back, never once has doing this really helped me overcome my issues. To a certain extent, it's human nature to be competitive, but God has also gifted us with the ability to control our thoughts and feelings. From the world's perspective, there will always be someone better than you, prettier than you, and richer than you. No matter how hard you try, you will never be enough. So why continue to beat yourself up and beat other innocent people up if it's never going to improve the situation? We have to somehow begin to realize that our own beauty is enough!

I am a Christian, and with this belief comes the comfort of knowing that I was created by the Creator of the universe who made me absolutely beautiful and in His image. However, I, too, often forget about what the meaning of real beauty is. On the days I feel the pressures of the world weighing on me, there are a few verses that I find of comfort.

"...The Lord does not look at the things man looks at. Man looks at the outward appearance, but the Lord looks at the heart." (NIV Study Bible,1 Samuel 16:7)

"For you created my inmost being; you knit me together in my mother's womb. I praise you because I am fearfully and wonderfully made; your works are wonderful, I know that full well. My frame was not hidden from you when I was made in the secret place. When I was woven together in the depths of the earth, your eyes saw my unformed body. All the days ordained for me were written in your book before one of them came to be." (NIV Study Bible, Psalm 139:13-16)

"Your beauty should not come from the outward adornment, such as braided hair and the wearing of gold jewelry and fine clothes. Instead, it should be that of your inner self, the unfading beauty of a gentle and quiet spirit, which is of great worth in God's sight. For this is the way the holy women of the past who put their hope in God used to make themselves beautiful..." (NIV Study Bible,1 Peter 3:3-5)

"Are not two sparrows sold for a penny? Yet not one of them will fall to the ground apart from the will of your Father. And even the very hairs of your head are all numbered. So don't be afraid; you are worth more than many sparrows." (NIV Study Bible, Matt 10:29-31)

"…because by one sacrifice he has made perfect forever those who are being made holy." (NIV Study Bible, Hebrews 10:14)

I know it's sometimes easy to read these verses or other types of encouraging words and think to yourself, "Aw, that's nice," and then not think anymore about it. But I challenge you to really think about what some of these words are telling you.

You are beautiful! God created you and knows every single strand of hair on your head! The Lord is the only One who will know your true beauty because He is the only one who knows what's in your soul. Why do we spend so many hours, days, and even years perfecting our outer appearances and yet spend such little time on our inner appearance?

My mom is one of the most beautiful women I have ever known—not only on the outside, but even more beautiful on the inside. She and my dad have been married for over thirty years. Appearance has always been of importance to my dad. He likes my mom's hair long. He likes that she stays fit and in shape. But now that my parents are getting older, he is beginning to realize even more why he loves my mom so much.

He has his own weight training business and is an active member of the community. We were recently talking about a lady who is physically absolutely beautiful. Based on outward appearances, you would think her husband would be fortunate to have her; however, about ten minutes after meeting her, my dad soon realized that her outer beauty did not correspond to inner beauty.

She was very condescending, would consistently cut people down—more than anyone, to her own husband—and had an all-around pessimistic attitude about life. The more my dad was around this woman the more he began reflecting on how thankful he was to be married to someone with a good heart and kind spirit. (Lucky for my dad, he got the best of both worlds; mom is just as beautiful inside as she is outside!) You see, although outward beauty may be attractive at first, it only runs skin deep…literally.

I'm going to put out a challenge for all you ladies, including myself. The next time you see someone who has the body you've always wanted or received the award you know you'll never get; instead of being jealous, read one of the verses above and tell yourself three things you like about yourself. Yes, three things. You can do it! Start with that and then give that person a smile or congratulations. I'll bet doing that will make you feel much better in the long run than that evil eye that might give you a minute or two of gratification.

And if you are on the receiving end of the evil eye or the rude comment, it's okay to stand up for yourself and allow your voice to be heard; however, I would encourage you to think carefully before you speak. If you make a comment back, is it really going to do any good? Are you really going to improve the situation by confronting this person?

Sometimes the answer is "yes," and other times the answer is "no." Sometimes you just have to smile and say to yourself, "They are just jealous of me," *because in all reality there is a good chance you've got something they don't have!*

2. Mountains Out of Molehills

Women can make mountains out of molehills. Let's be honest; we do. Take our relationship with our significant other, for example. When was the last time you got into an argument because your husband said you looked at him the wrong way? Or because he didn't feel connected with you at dinner? I'm going to take a wild guess and say it's not likely. Maybe it's happened in a few cases, but for the most part, guys are not usually the ones getting upset about a look or a "vibe."

God blessed women with intuition. Many times, we can see things or have a feeling about things before they happen. This is a true gift, and we should use this gift to help us make good decisions. However, sometimes Satan can twist this gift, and instead of using it as God intended, we can allow Satan to distort it for his own evil purposes.

I think we can all look back in our lives at a time we thought something about someone or judged someone negatively before knowing their story. I know there have been several times in my life when I've seen someone and thought a certain way about them because of the way they looked or because of what I'd heard about them from other people, only to realize I was 100% WRONG in my perception.

I challenge myself and my readers—next time you begin to take offense by a look or by a comment that has been made, step back and think to yourself, "Am I overreacting here? Is this person really judging me or insulting me? Am I being overly sensitive to things?" You may very well be right in your thinking, but step back before automatically assuming something because, in all reality, you may just be reading too much into it.

Let me conclude this chapter by imagining a world where women could look past their own insecurities and begin to encourage their fellow women instead of consistently comparing and judging them for simply "being a woman." Can you imagine the difference it would make in the world?

CHAPTER 7

Deja Vu

NOW THAT I'M in my 30s, I see things a little differently than I did in my teens, yet many of the same situations still exist. The only real difference is that the situations take place at work or in social settings instead of school. Even now though those left-out feelings can come back just like that without skipping a beat.

1. The Wedding: My husband and I recently attended a wedding for a friendly acquaintance. Although we knew quite a few of the guests, we ended up being "that couple" sitting in a corner by ourselves. A couple people came up to say "hi," but when it was time to sit down and eat dinner, everyone seemed to have somewhere else to sit. Although we had two extra seats across from us, everyone (including some members of our extended family) seemed to "find" somewhere else to sit. It's in these moments that I'm so thankful to have a "plus one" that will be my date forever.

While sitting there, I began to watch the people around me. After starting a family, my husband and I chose to move back to our hometown to raise our children. It's a wonderful rural community full of small town values, traditions, and a place where everyone knows your name. Because we are from a small town, most of the weddings or social events we attend involve people we grew up with and have known most of our lives. As I looked around the reception, it was almost comical to see the people I went to school with still acting like they were just that- in school.

They walked into the reception, threw their coats on a chair, and practically ran to the bar to begin what would end as a night in a drunken stupor. The next day they followed up with a social media replay bragging about how "wasted" they were the night before.

Then there were the parents of the people I went to school with, and unfortunately it was pretty easy to see where my former classmates learned their behavior. The parents were just as bad if not worse than the kids! They got their drinks and found "socially acceptable" friends to surround themselves with as they began their night of drinking and seeing who could be the center of attention.

Throughout the evening as I sat "people watching," I noticed that when a conversation involved just two women, it seemed to flow smoothly. But when a third woman approached the conversation without being invited, the dynamics shifted almost instantly. The ladies' body language changed almost immediately, from looking relaxed and casual to almost stoic with an "ice queen" vibe. The "newbie" immediately tried to immerse herself as if she had been a part of the conversation from the beginning. She laughed at appropriate times (or at least what she thought were the appropriate times). She would rub elbows with the ladies trying to send off the vibe that they were best buds, but in reality, she looked like nothing more than a fool to anyone watching for more than two minutes. It was very obvious to everyone that she was the odd woman out. She went on making herself look awkward by trying to socialize with these women even though it was obvious she was not welcome.

Now that I'm grown, it's funny to look at these women. These professional career-oriented women and parents—some even grandparents—still play the same game that they did in high school. They still invest an enormous amount of energy and effort into looking a part—a part that most of the time doesn't make them look any better; if anything, it makes them look like fools.

I don't get it. Why waste your energy on people who clearly don't accept or want you to be a part of their conversation (or life, for that matter)? And no matter how hard you try to fit in or brush off the feelings of insecurity, you know deep down that you're not welcome. You're not a part.

I know this, and I can sit here in the comfort of my own home and be comfortable saying this, yet in that moment at the wedding, there was still a significant part of me that silently cried out, "Come over here and sit by me. Really, I'm friendly! I want to talk to you!"

And as my husband and I sat in the corner that night, I decided just as I had in high school many times before, "Why stay and feel this icky feeling when we don't have to? Why force ourselves to remain in a situation that does nothing but make us feel bad?" We left right after dinner and went out for dessert. Being alone together became the highlight of the evening.

2. The Shower: I recently attended a baby shower and, like most showers I've gone to, there are usually some "go-to" people—you know, they're the ones who you already know and can quickly sit down with in order to avoid having to socialize with people you don't.

I found my go-tos and quickly sat down. I noticed a woman about three chairs down from me all by herself. I went to grab my food and came back to see a plate next to hers. "Oh, good," I thought to myself, "She has someone to talk to." And yet just as I was thinking that, I saw a lady come back, grab her plate and sheepishly grin before saying, "I saw Mary (or whoever) over there. I'm going to go sit by her." Looking a tad bit guilty, she smiled, gave a nervous laugh, grabbed her plate quickly and walked away. The woman who was left alone gave a half smile and nod, and then quickly looked down at her plate.

It wasn't hard to read her body language; it reminded me of a balloon that had just been deflated. Seriously? Talk about taking a person back to middle school in about 1.5 seconds—a grown woman leaving a table to sit by someone who is more "attractive" to her! This same deflated feeling came over me because I have been that deflated balloon many times. I was good enough to talk to when no one else was around, but not good enough to talk to when someone more appealing came along.

Think about the embarrassment of having others see a person leave you in favor of someone "better." Imagine that feeling, we've all felt it at some point in our lives, that feeling of being so alone in a room full of people.

Come on, ladies! Why do we do this to each other? Could this woman not have just invited her friend to join them? Perhaps because our own desire to be accepted is so strong, we totally forego any sense of politeness or self-awareness regarding how we make others feel.

Although part of our human nature wants to be around people with whom we are the most comfortable, it's also important to expand the way we think and interact even if it means having to consciously train ourselves to reflect in the moment about how our actions are making others feel. Even something as small as leaving a table can be incredibly hurtful to others.

As soon as I started a conversation with this woman, I saw her balloon begin to inflate again. She engaged in a conversation, moved her chair a little closer to mine, and smiled. That made going out of my comfort zone totally worth it!

For the majority of my life, I can honestly say I've tried to include people in my circle of friends. I know what it feels like to be left out and don't want to make others feel this way. However, as I say this, I must admit that the older I get, the more particular I am with who I will and won't offer my friendship to. Jaded? More than likely. And still today, even as I try so hard to be inclusive with my friendships, at times I get that icky feeling in the pit of my stomach when I see one of my friends starting to develop a close relationship with another person I introduced them to. I hope this feeling will go away as I get older, but so far, no luck.

3. Mommy group: There is a mommy group that I'm involved in, and I love getting together with other moms and being able to have some adult conversation in the midst of changing diapers and being spit up on. But I have noticed at times that when a new woman joins us, there is that small part of me that is reluctant to accept that person into the group.

Don't get me wrong, mommy group gals—I love all the ladies in our group! But I think I react this way because I still have a fear that I will end up being left out. I'm sure that a psychologist could totally have a field day with why I am the way I am about these things, but the best explanation I can give is that I want to hold on to friends with a tight grip because of the fear that by loosening my grip even a little, these friends will slip away.

In the process of writing this book, I interviewed several women of all ages to gain different perspectives on their experiences, both in school and as adults. One middle aged woman I interviewed— we will call her "Heidi"—shared an all-too-common situation. Heidi had an old high school friend—we will call her "Jackie"—who had children who were the same age as Heidi's children. Both lived in the same town, and both of their children were involved in basketball. It was very common for both Jackie and Heidi to be in the same place at the same time. A lot of people Heidi considered friends would sit with Jackie at the games. It didn't take very long before it became apparent that Heidi was not welcome to sit with Jackie or her "friends" at the games. It was the same high school games playing out as adults. You know what I'm talking about. It's the looking the other way when they see the person approaching, scooting the purse over so they don't have room to sit, interrupting the middle of a conversation to talk to someone else. All the typical teenage mean girl stuff except these were grown women.

Heidi couldn't understand why these women would be like this to her. She was very upset and even admitted that she went home and cried. (Now, keep in mind that this is a very successful woman with an absolutely wonderful family, beautiful home, good career, and admits to having many very good friends, yet this situation caused her immense pain.) It only took one woman to manipulate a small group of people into believing that Heidi was not a worthy person. Twenty-five years after high school, all the same feelings came right back as if it were yesterday.

These situations are not going away, no matter how old we get. In some ways, I believe that God puts us in these situations as parents to remind us of how it made us feel when we were teenagers, so that we are able to relate to our children going through these same feelings now. The difference is, as adults we can opt out of a situation in many cases. It's not that easy when you are a teenager in school all day dealing with the same people every day and unable to disconnect.

Nowadays, even when your child gets home, there is no real disconnection because of social media. Our children are constantly reminded of their status in the world (or what they think is their status). It can come in so many different forms, from someone not liking their latest Snapchat, to being deleted as a friend on Facebook, to looking at an Instagram post of all the people you thought were your friends at some place you weren't invited to.

The difference between being a teenager and not feeling like you belong and being an adult with the same feeling is this: as a teenager you don't have the life experience yet to put these situations into perspective. And it's hard when you're surrounded by the same people all day, every day.

Although the surroundings may be a little different if you go to a school that's larger than my school—there were less than 150 in my graduating class—many of the dynamics are the same. Students are frequently surrounded by the same group of classmates throughout their high school experience. If you are an athlete, you spend the majority of your time with other athletes at school, games, practices, etc. It may not necessarily be because these are the types of people you really enjoy being around (although sometimes this is the case), but it's because your interests are the same. You are somewhat required to be together whether you like it or not. In school (especially in smaller ones), you can't just leave and go to a different cafeteria for lunch. You can't go to a different building for class in order to remove yourself from certain situations. In my case, this made me feel trapped, like no matter what, I was consistently surrounded by people with whom I didn't want to associate.

That being said, as an adult, although you may still have to deal with people you don't care for at times, it's much easier to remove yourself from situations that make you feel uncomfortable because you are not "stuck"—and I mean this both figuratively and literally. Most of you have vehicles and can physically leave a situation if you need to. We also have some experience under our belts and can more accurately perceive a situation for what it is and what it isn't. We can therefore evaluate if it is worth keeping ourselves in the situation or if it's better to remove ourselves altogether. And even if you do have to be around unappealing people, for example in Heidi's situation, you don't have to associate with them. You don't have to sit with them, talk to them, try to fit into their "mold" of what you should be. And while parents may be able to *effortlessly* tell their teenage daughter, "Oh just go sit somewhere else." or, "don't worry about what they say about you; just ignore it." If you think back it will only take most parents a very short time to remember that in those teenage years this is sometimes almost impossible to do.

As an adult it is incredibly refreshing when I am in a group that I don't necessarily feel right in, instead of feeling "yucky" about it, I am able to make the conscious decision to be the one left out. It's that simple. I walk away and take myself out of the situation altogether. I'm the one that makes the decision to leave instead of being left out of it by others. Let me tell you, ladies, walking away can be such a great feeling!

As parents, we need to remind our children they are not alone, share with them experiences we've had of being left out, of feeling alone in a group of people. They need to know that their parents DO understand where they're coming from. If you are a Christian, I would also encourage you to remind your child of something my mom always reminded me of:

*** I remember when you were struggling the most with feeling lonely and rejected that I continued to assure you that no matter how lonely you felt, you were never alone. I told you that God is always right there with you and will NEVER leave you or betray you and that He cares more about you than anyone. We would talk about how God understands how you feel and that he was rejected and betrayed more than anyone, to the point of death. I remember telling you that although I don't understand why you have to go through such a difficult time, I truly believed that God was in control and he would someday use your trials for good and for His glory. He was molding you into a young woman with a sensitive heart for those who are rejected and felt alone.***

And can I just add one more thing for the girls out there? You know that phrase, "high school is the best time of your life"? When I was younger, I remember hearing that and thinking to myself, "Great, if this is the best time of my life, then I hate to see how the rest of my life will turn out." Most of the time this is not the case—high school is not necessarily the best time of your life. In fact, high school can be awful! But trust me, it does get better! As one of the young women I interviewed said, "All bad things are temporary."

Let me end this chapter with a challenge. The next time you are in a room with a group of friends, make a conscious effort to find someone sitting alone, someone who looks out of place in the room. Go up to her; start a conversation; sit next to her. Venture out of your comfort zone. Push aside the feeling that by leaving your group you may "miss" something.

Don't feel scared of what it may do to your own status or comfort level. Think about how you would feel if you were the person alone in a room full of people. You never know the impact of a few kind words or what sitting next to someone can do for them. You could be the best thing that happened to them that day.

Come on, ladies, take the chance! Be aware! Be the difference in someone's day. Really, isn't seeing someone change their whole demeanor because of you worth it? Be the change in their day. It may just change yours, as well!

CHAPTER 8

The Book Club Cover

WE ARE RELATIONAL people. God made us that way. He made Eve to give Adam someone to talk to, to share with, to love. He created us with the need for companionship whether that be a husband, wife, friend or even a pet. (In my case, I have Hank, a.k.a. the best dog EVER!)

My first job after college graduation was at a state university. I worked for the International Student and Scholar Services office. One of the first stops international students made upon their arrival was to our office.

You could tell very quickly who the newly arriving students were. They were the ones fumbling around, trying to get all their admissions documents in order, looking around anxiously at all of the new scenery as they waited in line. During admissions week, the entire front of our lobby was filled with pamphlets, signs, advertisements, and student ambassadors waiting to tell the new students about different campus organizations they could join.

Interestingly enough, although these students were coming from all around the globe to a small town in the middle of a corn field (literally!) for an education, I didn't see too many of them eager to see where their economics class would be held. Instead, as soon as they saw that there was a paintball club, Tang Soo Do club, Competitive Super Smash Brothers Club, or whatever their interest was, their eyes seemed to light up and their attention was drawn that way.

Was it because there was a group dedicated to dipping things in chocolate? (Yes, that really was the focus of a club!) Maybe. My guess, however, is that they were more interested in becoming a part of a group where they could feel accepted and relate to others around them. Whether they had come from 100 miles away or 10,000 miles away, these students were looking for the same thing: relationships, community, and acceptance.

As adults, the need for relationships doesn't go away. At this particular phase in my life (early 30s) book clubs have become trendy social events. The group members choose a book, read a couple of chapters each week, and then come together to chat about their thoughts on the book.

How many of you have been to a book club where you actually talk about the book you are reading? How many of you have even actually read the book? If you answer "yes," then great for you! But most book clubs that I know of are more like social get-togethers, sometimes even involving a glass or two of wine (if you're lucky!). Many times, the book isn't even mentioned at the gathering.

There is nothing at all wrong with this; in fact, if you're a mom with young kids like me, sometimes it's exactly what you need! However, you're not in the club because you like to read the book—well, maybe you do—but my point is that you are there because you're a relational being. Who doesn't want someone to talk to, to listen to, to share things with? Like I said before, there is nothing wrong with wanting to be accepted; when it becomes dangerous is when we allow ourselves to be consumed with acceptance so much that we forget or change who we are in the process.

One girl in my 8th grade class comes to mind. She was always about number six or seven in the royal court. Sometimes she jumped ahead to four or five if one of the girls slipped up and got in trouble with the queen. I remember thinking to myself, "Why does this poor girl make such a fool of herself every day trying so hard to fight her way in without ever really succeeding?"

It was before I'd become a member of the royal court, and there were a couple of times in particular that I remember her coming over to us commoners. She would be upset and tell us how mean these girls were to her and how she didn't understand why they would treat her like this. The girls in our group would gather around her and rally for her, giving her the attention and support she so desperately craved. The sad thing was that most of the group wasn't doing this because they were genuinely concerned for her. They did it because if they became her friend, it might bump them up a couple spots from where they were. So pathetic, I know, but that's how it was.

I remember one time asking this girl, "Why do you feel like you have to be friends with people who treat you so badly?" I can't remember her answer, but it must not have mattered too much because every time she would cry to us, it was only a day or two before we no longer existed for her again. She would be right back circling the court, waiting for an opening so she could slide back in as if she had never left.

This girl never really changed. All the way up into high school—and even beyond—she still tried to make it into that coveted royal court. She never really succeeded, but she did everything in her power to make other people think she had.

Just within the last couple of years, we have become friends on social media. While looking at her profile, I found it very interesting that after almost fifteen years out of school, her profile pic wasn't of her with her family, children, or even just of her. Her picture showed her with a couple of the royal court members that she strived so hard to be friends with in high school but that never really accepted her (at least not back then)!

So, after all these years, has something changed? Have these women finally accepted her for the person she really is? I truly hope so for her sake; however, I hope even more that this woman is not still trying to be accepted by people around which she could never be her genuine self. This is an issue I see so many women dealing with today, and it spans no age limit. I have been this person at times in my life, and it makes me sad and ashamed when I look back at the times

I have allowed myself to hide the person I really was for the sake of acceptance.

I am very fortunate, though, to have made the decision in 8th grade to stop allowing others to dictate who I should be, how I should act, dress, talk, laugh, etc. and just be who God made me to be. Was it hard? Absolutely! Sitting by myself at lunch, on the bus, spending my weekends at home because I didn't get invited to go out to things--It sucked. There is no nice way of putting it! Did I have slip ups? Of course! How could I not? There would be times I was so lonely I would conform for short periods of time in order to get a small amount of acceptance but it wouldn't last long before that voice in my head would remind me that what I was doing was wrong and not worth it. In reality, being a teenager is really such a short period of your life. You'll never regret being your self in the long run. What you may regret, though, is not being who you genuinely are.

CHAPTER **9**

Angels in Your Midst

I TRULY BELIEVE with all of my heart that God puts certain people into our lives for a reason. With some, it's for a season; with others, it's for a lifetime. I was very blessed to have three friends who, in addition to my wonderful family, helped me through these years.

God also provided me with what my mom and I describe as an "angel" who took me under her wing.

> *** God provided a secretary named Mary who literally took you under her "angel" wings and provided a safe place for you to talk, sit at lunch, or go to whenever things were really tough. Mary was also the cheerleading coach, and I think she was the one that encouraged you to try out for cheerleading.*
>
> *So we turned our living room into a gymnasium for a few months, and I still remember your dad trying to teach you how to do a cartwheel. I watched you do countless cheers over and over again. Sure enough, by God's grace, you made the squad. However, what we had hoped to be a great ex-perience soon turned out to be one of the worst because cheerleaders were some of the most popular girls in school, and they did not seem to appreciate the new competition. Although they were never deliberately cruel or mean to you, they seemed to make sure you knew you were not part of the*

group, and because of this attitude, they used exclusion to try to bring you down.

For whatever reason, maybe pride, you were determined not to let them succeed, yet you were not willing to play their games either, so you held your head high in their presence and then came home and cried almost every night. I knew you were lonely and wanted nothing more than one good friend. I remember encouraging you and telling you that popular is just a word. Most of the girls who were popular were really just very lonely girls trying to "stay in the popular group." I urged you to seek out friends who were not in the "popular" group.

After that, I remember when you reached out and became friends with a girl named Jill. Although she was about a polar opposite from you, she didn't care how she looked or what people thought of her; she accepted you just the way you were. About that time, you also met your first real "boyfriend," Mark, who really became your "best friend." He was funny, popular, witty, and always knew how to make you laugh. He really was your saving grace; it no longer mattered what the girls thought of you, you had a friend. Although he may not have been the "love of your life," he was your friend and accepted you for who you really were. ***

I could have never imagined that the guy I started dating my sophomore year would be the person I'd consider my best friend and confidant for the next four years of my life. Unlike me, when we started dating, he was very popular and charismatic. He had lots of friends and was the life of the party. I don't exactly remember how he first caught my attention, but I do remember one area of attraction being that he wasn't concerned that I didn't belong to the same group he did.

He didn't care that I wasn't popular or didn't have the same friends he did. He wasn't concerned that by dating me he may not "move up" the social ladder. He loved me for me. The real me. He accepted me the way I was, overly sensitive and all.

Sometimes he was the only reason I would get up and go to school in the morning. To see him waiting with a genuine love and warmth at my locker as I arrived was something I had never had in a friend before. Although there was a romantic side to our relationship, as I look back, I can see how he was so much more of a friend to me than anything else. He never tried to change me or influence me to be someone other than the person I was.

Ladies, let me tell you—if you are in a relationship where you feel like you have to put on a façade around the person you are with, you need to run away very fast. You can only pretend to be someone you aren't for so long. You don't want to be with someone who you can't genuinely be yourself around. I promise you, you will not regret leaving.

Although our relationship didn't work out and we have moved on from each other, he is someone I will always think of with love and appreciation for allowing me to be myself. A quote from William Shakespeare comes to mind when I think of our relationship and what he was to me, "A friend is one who knows who you are, understands where you have been, accepts what you have become and still gently allows you to grow." That is the true definition of a friend, and that is what he was to me.

There was another significant "angel" that was brought into my life around the time I was in the 4th grade. Mr.H was a grandfather figure to me and still is. He was an incredible godly man who went to our church, and my mom suggested that we become prayer partners when I was about eleven years old. To this day, although we are hundreds of miles apart, we try to keep in contact with one another and pray together over the phone every now and then.

This man was and still is such a place of solace for me. The picture of him is so clear in my mind. He sat in his rocking chair, hands folded with a peaceful smile, rocking back and forth as he listened to me share my innermost struggles and battles with him. He, in turn, would share his prayer requests with me. I never once felt him judge me, and he always seemed to give me godly wisdom and advice without making me feel like he was trying to "parent" me.

One day I remember going to visit him, and while sitting outside in the garden, I admitted to him that I had thought about hurting my-self. I had never told anyone these thoughts before, but I knew that if I could tell anyone, I could tell him. I had never seen him cry before that day. I knew he genuinely loved me and was concerned about what I was feeling. He talked with me, and we prayed.

Before I left, he gave me a small sandstone rock. He told me that it was something he always carried with him while growing up and that whenever he was having a hard time, he would look at it and it gave him some type of comfort. He wanted me to have it, and every time I looked at it, he wanted me to know someone was praying for me and that things would get better.

That is something that stuck with me forever. Such a small gesture had such a significant impact on me. To have some type of physical reminder that I was being thought of and prayed for throughout the day gave me a sense of peace that helped me through some of my darkest days.

*When your children are old enough, find an older person within your church that you trust and that believes God's principles. Ask him/her to be a prayer partner for your child. There will be times when your child doesn't want to tell you everything; however, if they have a prayer partner that they trust and can talk to, then you know that they are getting good godly advice. You had a wonderful prayer partner that met with you weekly, and I was so thankful that you had someone else to go to that you could share your concerns with. I could trust Mr.H was giving you good sound direction which was better than you going to some of your peers who might not have been giving you the best advice/direction.***

When helping your teenagers through their struggles, sometimes there is only so much a parent can do. Sometimes it helps to have another trusted adult that they can go to without fear. I'm so thankful my mom was intuitive enough to know that Jerry would be a blessing to me, not only as someone to meet with for prayer, but also as a mentor and friend. It gave her someone she was able to trust 100% to give me godly advice and care for me in the same loving way she did.

At the same time, it gave me someone I could talk to about things that I may not have wanted my mom to know about or felt she would not understand. It was such a blessing for everyone involved.

Sometimes one person is all it takes to really make a difference. I was blessed enough to have three.

CHAPTER **10**

A Mother's Perspective

AS I'VE SAID again and again, my mom was my rock. More than anyone else, she was the person that got me through this period of my life. Each day, every day, she was the one that was there. She saw me at both my best and worst moments. She would come into my room every night and many nights hold me while I cried in her arms and told her I couldn't do it anymore. She had to watch as I fell deeper and deeper into a depressed state. She was the one who went with me to the doctor to get the medical attention I needed to treat my depression and anxiety. She was the one who picked me up from school at lunch time so I could get out of there, even if it was for just thirty minutes.

I know there were days she didn't want to hear me cry or complain about what drama had upset me, but never once—let me repeat, NEVER ONCE—did she tell me she didn't want to hear about it. NEVER ONCE did she tell me she didn't have time to listen. NEVER ONCE did she tell me my feelings weren't validated. NEVER ONCE.

I thank God for that, for if she had even once said one of these things, I truly fear that it could have been my last day on this earth. As a mother now I can't even imagine some of what my mother had to go through with me. How was she able to deal with all of my difficulties, and yet continue to have a positive outlook every day? I asked her about this as I was writing.

*** It was a very difficult time. When you are a mom, you feel what your children feel—maybe even more than they do. As a teenager, school was difficult for me, but it was even harder watching my own child go through it. As a mom, we want to "fix" it for our kids, but we can't always do that, we have to provide them with tools to take care of themselves. Trying to provide a balance of guiding you without doing it for you was hard. If I had not had such a strong faith in God and an instruction manual called "the Bible" as my guide, I honestly don't know how I would have gotten through it. It wasn't just some book giving me good advice, it was my truth that I believe in. I never questioned what it said because I know it was true.

I also had a wonderful support system—a husband who would balance me when I would want to do too much for you girls. He also took care of most of our financial needs so that I could be at home when you got home from school and be here for you both.

I had a strong group of Christian friends who helped me and taught me how to be a Christian parent. When you were younger, I would get you both tucked into bed, and then a group of us would go and walk for an hour and talk about what was going on with our families and support one another. As you got older, I would get up early in the morning and walk and do the same. They were wonderful friends who allowed me to share my deepest feelings, thoughts and concerns and were willing to tell me when I was not thinking correctly. They were my spiritual mothers and sisters.

I never really thought about it until now, but maybe that is why still to this day, walking is such an important part of my day. Most importantly, what probably helped me the most *was that I prayed a lot. I would get up early, spend time with God and pray for you girls, then I'd pray throughout the day and at night before I went to sleep I prayed over all that went on throughout the day.****

Although I am a mother myself now, I have yet to deal with a child going through adolescence. Because my mom is such a large part of my story I wanted her to share her thoughts and perspectives on that time in life and what her feelings were through it all.

***Junior high started at our little cottage school at our church. It was a place where you felt safe for the most part. A place where you felt like you were somebody and could explore your adolescence and start to figure out who you were.

School was hard for you. Learning was difficult and took longer for you than for most, so the cottage school was a good fit. You got a lot of individual attention and time.

You also were able to seek out your own interests. I remember when you wanted to be a singer like Reba McEntire. You'd put on shows and dress up in your fancy dresses, and your peers came alongside you to sing back up. We encouraged your dreams by getting you private singing lessons.

Then we decided 8th grade would be a good time to start the transition back into public school. We had hoped it would be a smooth transaction. I'm afraid it was not. Going from a class room of sixteen 8th graders into a school of over 100 8th graders from all backgrounds was a big change.

I knew you were terrified to walk into that school each day. It was so hard to take you and drop you off each day; it felt like I was giving you to the wolves to devour you, but I also knew you had to adjust to the "world" and prayed every day that you would be strong enough to do so.

At the beginning, you were terrified. I remember you coming home telling me stories about kids you thought had guns or weapons and used terrible language. You felt excluded and lonely. I was pretty sure the guns and weapons were an issue only in your imagination, and the language was something I knew you could overcome. But the feelings of loneliness and feeling unaccepted by those who had already established their "pecking" order was almost unbearable. I did a lot of praying that year and was determined to help you succeed, so again, the goal was to find what your interests were and to focus on your goals and give it all you had. Everyone needs a purpose and goals, and that was always something I tried to instill in you.

You continued to enjoy singing, and so we continued with music lessons and were so blessed to become friends with the music teacher. We learned that she, too, was a Christian. It was a safe place for you to go when things were tough. We also had spent a lot of time playing volleyball with our church, and you decided you wanted to try out for the team. Pretty much every night after dinner we went outside or over to the park and played volleyball. We took advantage of anyone and everyone, from friends to cousins, to come alongside you and work with you to help you succeed. It would be really hard to make the volleyball team since you didn't play your 7ᵗʰ grade year, but it gave you a goal, a purpose, and something through which I could support you in every way possible. Whether you made the team or not, we knew you gave it everything you had.

I knew that school continued to be hard for you and that

every day was difficult, but you were learning to "get through it." During those days I started a group of prayer warriors that met before school every week to pray for you, the school, the teachers and the junior high kids. We became friends with some of the teachers, so we knew more specifically how to pray and what the needs were, and then we would make them treats to encourage them as they attempted to teach and mentor the students.

God was good, and after hours of practicing volleyball, your hard work paid off. One of the highlights of 8th grade was the day you found out you had made the volleyball team. Also, by the end of your 8th grade year, you won an award for the top female singer. God was so good to bless you and encourage you through a difficult year. I know you never felt like you fit in with the other girls, and I believe you never even felt like you had a truly good friend, but thankfully there were things that happened that encouraged you and kept you going. It breaks my heart to think of so many who don't have those little blessings.

HIGH SCHOOL

We were looking forward to high school, and I remember I kept trying to encourage you by telling you high school gets better. The cattiness of girls starts to settle down, and they don't focus so much on bringing each other down. They start to settle in and accept each other where they are. Again, I encouraged you to find what you were good at and what you really liked and give it everything you had to try to make it happen.

You continued with music, which was a place where I believe you felt safe and accepted for the most part. You also realized the fact that you had "developed" at a much younger age than most of your peers. You recognized this as an advantage because although you didn't get the acceptance of the girls, you did get the attention of the boys.

This was by far probably one of our biggest trials during your high school years—the way you dressed and the image you were portraying to others. You had the body of a 20-year-old as a 14-15-year-old girl. I believe you decided to use this to your advantage, and if the girls weren't going to accept you, then at least the boys did.

You decided to make your mark by wearing dresses and dressing up almost every day. If your peers weren't going to make you feel good about yourself, you would just do it yourself. You carried yourself well and walked confidently with a smile on your face so that others didn't see the hurt that was really deep within you. However, the harder you tried to portray that you were confident and happy, the more the girls seemed to try to bring you down and ignore you to make sure you knew that was not the case***

Tell me what your feelings were when I would come home upset. What went through your head?

***To be honest, there was a mixture of emotions. There was anger, frustration, intense pain, a breaking heart, fear of what you would do, wanting to fix it but wanting you to grow as well, doubting my own advice.

Intense pain for you: indescribable. Despite everything I went through in junior high and high school, the pain I felt for you going through it was ten times greater because you were my daughter. I wanted to do anything to take that pain away.

Watching you go through similar feelings to what I had in school brought back a lot of feelings that I had tried to forget. However, now I wasn't in control of the situation, and I could only do my best to guide you through it and stand beside you. I was so thankful to be able to work jobs where I could be at home when you walked in the door so you could talk and cry, and I could encourage and uplift you and listen to you and hug you.

A breaking heart: I couldn't take the pain away from you. As a parent, whenever our children are hurt or sad or having a rough day, we pick them up, love them, have a special day with them, or make them laugh. A lot of times their problems seem to disappear.

This changes with time, and as our children grow, the severity of the issues seem to rise. For example, a younger child may be upset because someone took a toy away that he or she was playing with. Although it is a big deal to the child in the moment, it's also a very minor emotional hurdle to overcome. Usually focusing attention elsewhere for a period of time will be sufficient in overcoming that issue.

It becomes harder as our children get older because their emotions and capacity to see beyond the immediate future intensifies, which allows longer lasting, more passionate feelings and emotions. No longer will a piece of candy and a happy song negate the feelings they are having.

There were days when no matter what I did, I knew I couldn't fix it; you would have to walk right back into the same thing the next day. I would spend hours praying for you throughout the day that God would get you through another day and bless you with something positive in your day--a light that you could see and find hope in, and amazingly He did this over and over again.

Fear of what you would do: There were days when you'd cry yourself to sleep and wake up crying, saying you just couldn't do it again. You would call me during the day from school and tell me you were having a panic attack and had to get out of the building. I would agree to pick you up from lunch on the condition that you would return for the afternoon, but it gave you a break from the pain.

I was so fearful at one time of what you were thinking—I was pretty sure you were considering suicide or hurting yourself—and I was so desperate that I read your diary. I was right; you had made a comment that you "would rather be in the hospital than go to school."

I had a long talk with you, and we made an agreement that if things ever got so bad that you considered hurting herself that you would call me and we would come get you. We would figure out an alternative, even if it meant a private school. You made a promise, and I trusted you to keep it.

Wanting to fix it but wanting you to grow as well: I remember so badly just wanting to fix it for you. I wanted to just march into that school and take you out and home school you and keep you safe inside our four little walls, but I knew that if I did that, I would keep you from growing and learning how to deal with circumstances in life. That is why when we would plan alternatives if things got so bad that you could not handle it, I never offered to homeschool. It was the easy way out.

I also knew deep within me that God was using this for His plan. I truly believed He was allowing these things to happen *so that someday you would use your experiences for His pur-pose. I wasn't sure if it would be to help others or to teach you true empathy and compassion for those who were struggling, but I believed without a doubt He would use this in some way if you could learn to work through it.****

After homecoming parade and rally where I was announced senior homecoming queen.

Prom picture senior year after being announced prom queen.

My dad & I dancing at homecoming.

From left: My(Now husband) Brad, me, my sister-Tessa, my mom-Wendy, and my dad-Bret.

Easter picture with mom and Tessa.

Senior football cheerleading.   *My "best friend" Tyson Ali.*

Another family pic.

Junior year prom.

PART 2
REFLECTIONS

We have looked at my experience from different angles, but now I want us to get down to the nitty-gritty practical things that mothers can put into practice that will help us support and encourage our kids as they go through these difficult times.

CHAPTER **11**

The Power of Being Present

I'VE SEEN IT time after time (and I must admit I am guilty at times, as well): a parent whose child is trying to have a conversation with him/her and the parent is on the phone, blatantly ignoring the child. I recently watched a father and son have dinner at a restaurant where literally *zero* words were spoken. The son spent the entire dinner on his phone while the father sat and stared blankly into space. Never once did either try to start up a conversation.

Time after time, this lack of communication has played out between parents and children, and time after time, I've seen the looks of disappointment and sadness in both the parent's and child's face when they are being ignored because of a text, a phone call, a snapchat, or _____ (you fill in the blank). I am not naive to the society we live in, and I know that social media is a way of life for almost everyone. But let me remind us (including myself) that our children are watching us and taking mental notes on how we engage them. Our interaction with them then influences the way our children interact with others. Some parents are so disconnected from their children that even though they have good intentions and want to have a good relationship with their children, they don't know where to start.

A college friend recently shared a story with me about a girl she knew—we will call her Jess—who was struggling with being accepted and was feeling excluded by her peers. Her mom had a hard time connecting with Jess because her own teenage experience had been very different. Jess's mom loved school, had a lot of friends, and was a cheerleader. In other words, she basically had the ideal teenage experience. Her mother was determined to make Jess fit in. In her mind, if Jess was "popular," her social problems would be solved.

Jess wanted to be on the basketball team more than anything. She went to camps, practiced at home, went to open gyms, and did everything she could to make the team. Her mom decided to "encourage" her by telling Jess that she would buy her a new iPhone if she made the team.

The day of tryouts came, and Jess nailed it! She was so excited about how well things had gone that she took pictures after tryouts, posted on social media, and called some of her family members to tell them about what had happened. For one of the first times in her life, she felt proud of herself. She just *knew* she would make the team, yet she waited for what seemed like an eternity until the list of new team members was finally posted later that night.

Jess made her way through the crowd of girls all vying for the first look at the dry eraser board with a list of names. She scanned the list, looking for that name she had written so many times, but she couldn't find it. She looked again. Still no name.

Finally, the truth hit her, and she turned away, tears beginning to well up in her eyes as she walked toward the door. Through the blur, Jess saw girls cheering and hugging, jumping up and down as they congratulated each other, but she couldn't bear to look at any of them. All she could think about was getting out of that building.

She opened the car door only to see the look of excitement on her mom's face immediately change to disappointment. Devastated didn't even begin to describe Jess's feelings. Not only had she not been good enough to make the team, not only did her hard work not pay off, not only was she embarrassed by her brief burst of confidence, but now she felt she had let down the most influential person in her life—her mother. And to add salt to the wound, Jess wouldn't even be receiving the reward her mom had promised her if she made the team.

Although I truly believe Jess's mom had the best of intentions when she added to the pressure on Jess, it became much harder for Jess when she didn't accomplish her goal. While I understand the concept of encouragement through reward, and I don't necessarily disagree with it on certain occasions, one of the worst things a mother can do to her daughter's self-confidence is give her conditional affirmation.

Jess needed to know that she was already a winner in her mother's eyes, that no matter what, her mom was proud of her for all the effort she had put in. If only her mom would have told her these things out loud, face-to-face, eye-to-eye! Getting the iPhone wasn't what Jess really wanted. Sure, it would have been nice, but what she was striving for more than anything else was to feel accepted (probably by her mom more than anyone). She needed a safe place to land. Instead, she was crushed once again by feelings of exclusion, failure, and rejection.

As parents, sometimes we decide we need to "fix" things and take it upon ourselves to do what we think is best in our own minds instead of being present both physically and emotionally in our child's life. Hearing what they have to say is so important. Let me spell it out even more clearly—hearing what they have to say **without distraction is SOOO important!** Maybe if Jess's mom would have spent more time listening to her daughter's verbal and non-verbal signals she may have been better able to know how to encourage her. She may have realized that what Jess needed more than anything was her mother's acceptance for who she was, not acceptance for what she could (or could not) accomplish.

You'll never know what your child may have shared with you if you hadn't taken the call, or finished reading the post. Think about the last time you were with someone, sharing something personal with them, and then in the middle of the conversation, they picked up their phone. How did that make you feel?

Unimportant? Not a priority? Exactly. Guess what? Your children feel the same way!

CHAPTER **12**

Listen & Learn

WHILE WRITING THIS book I interviewed several females ranging from five years old (that would be my daughter, Tinley, who didn't want to miss out on being part of the book!) to women in their 70s. I asked them lots of questions about their teenage experience. One of the questions asked was if they had parents they felt they could talk to about the struggles they faced growing up. Here are some of the most common responses I received.

"I feel like a burden...I'll say something and she'll be watching the game."

"I wish they would have been more involved."

"I wish my mom would have been more willing to talk about the struggles I was having. I think she held me to a standard of [perfection]. I always felt I was disappointing her in some way."

"She [my mother] listens to me but will try to give me advice while I'm talking. It's frustrating."

"I don't have a relationship in which I feel like I can trust my parents. I think they would tell their friends [about my

struggles]. Sometimes when I tell them things, they think I'm just faking it. I don't think my parents really care."

I interviewed several mom/daughter duos in my research for this book. They were interviewed separately, and often the mothers' and daughters' perceptions of their relationship varied dramatically. Many of the moms thought they had pretty open relationships with their children; however, when I interviewed the daughters, they had a very different perspective. Again, while not an expert, I *have* learned quite a bit from my own mom, as well as from other mothers I've grown up around and interviewed. That being said, what is the secret to raising successful, happy daughters in a world full of drama, competition, and mean girls? How can mothers and daughters so frequently mis-understand their own relationship? And how do we fix that?

I'm sure most caring, loving parents would like to say their children can talk to them about anything. But when it comes down to it this is much easier said than done, especially with teenagers. It's even more challenging if you have never really had an open dialogue with them in their younger years about the easy stuff. Then how do you jump to the harder discussions from really no base line? Well, I can tell you it's probably not going to be easy, but then again what part of parenting is? I'd like to address a few areas that may help you and your children begin the steps toward removing the communication roadblocks that so often seem to get in the way in the parent-child relationship.

1. Ask Your Children Questions and LISTEN to Their Answers.

When you pick your kids up from an event, drive around for a little while; take the long way home and take advantage of this undivided time with your kids. You have to be there at the moment things take place because that's when they are the most excited or upset and will talk about it.

73

Spend time together as a family every day. Have meals to-gether, talk at the table, ask A LOT of questions even if they seem silly. Your kids may laugh at you, but they really do love knowing that you want to hear what they have to say.

Every day when I pick my daughter, Tinley, up from school, the first thing I ask is, "How was your day?" Most of the time, I get the same answer: "Good." So I realized very early in her life that ask-ing specific questions was key. By this, I mean questions that require more than a yes/no answer, questions that I know are related to things that are important to her day. "Who brought show and tell? What did they bring?" "What did you have for a snack?" "Who did you play with and what did you play?" "What was your favorite thing about your day?" "What was the worst thing about your day?"

Now granted, my daughter is in pre-school, so the types of ques-tions I ask her are usually not extremely in-depth. However, by open-ing up dialogue at an early age, it naturally allows our children to become comfortable with the idea of sharing things. It also helps them realize, even if in a subconscious way, that what they are saying is important to their parents.

But wait. Asking questions is just the first part, and also usually the easiest. The second part—which is often much harder for us par-ents—is listening to their answers.

Next time you ask your child a question, make a conscious effort to ask yourself, "Am I really listening to what she is saying or am I just waiting for her to finish so I can talk again? Or am I thinking about what to make for dinner? The tough conference call at work today? The fact that I forgot to take cookies to the bake sale yesterday and now I feel like all 'those' moms are giving me the evil eye?"

Here's one I've seen and have to admit to doing before—taking a phone call in the middle of a conversation with your child. Sometimes it can seem like second nature to pick up the phone as soon as we hear the ding from a text or the vibration of a call. We don't even think for a second about how responding to the phone could make a difference in listening to a two-minute conversation your child is having about how she didn't get picked first at P.E. that day.

Trust me—it makes a difference! Elevating distractions and focusing solely on what your child is saying lets them know that, if nothing else, they are your priority. Being present with them invites an atmosphere of trust, communication, and love.

I would like to encourage parents who are reading this to make intentional choices about the distraction level in your lives. For the next thirty days, I challenge you to make your children the priority in your life for at least thirty minutes.

Yes, I know. Most of you are going to say, "My children are consistently my priority. I'm either feeding them, helping with homework, or taking them to practice."

But this is different. This exercise requires you to put your phone/computer/tablet/etc. literally out of sight. Put it in a place where you cannot be tempted by minor distractions. Although ideally, I believe the best time to do this is when your children get home from school, timing isn't always the most important factor. You must make it a routine part of the day.

Thirty minutes of undivided attention—if your children want to play outside, play outside with them. If they want to go to DQ for ice cream, take them there and eat together. Do whatever you need to do to show them they have your attention.

Try it for thirty days and see if you can tell a difference in the communication level you have with your child. The first couple of days might be a little strange, especially if you're the type of family who sits with their head glued to their phones during dinner, but after a few repetitive interactions (preferably at the same time each day), you may be surprised at just how open your children may become.

Making this a priority when your children are young makes it easier when they are older because they already recognize communication as a normal, everyday thing that just happens. Therefore, they will be more likely to share with you the things going on in their lives.

And if you're a parent for whom this concept is totally new, don't get frustrated. This is a process like everything else.

In an article written in the *European Journal of Social Psychology* a study was done by Phillippa Lally to show how long it takes to form a new habit. Lally's research showed that it took anywhere from 18 to 254 days to get to a point of automaticity. In other words, building communication with your children may take a while, so don't give up too quickly!

Think of it this way: You have gone to work every day for the last ten years to the same desk in the same office. You have your morning routine of setting down your things, grabbing your coffee, turning up the thermostat—it's always freezing in offices!—and checking your email. Same thing. Each day. Ten years.

Then one day you walk into your office, and your desk is gone. You look around and see that the whole office has been rearranged. After a slight panic, you find your desk, but the area where you usually set your things has already been taken by someone else. The thermostat is now located in the next room, and the coffee maker in this room is not the same one that you have been using for the last ten years. What in the world has your life become!

Although rearranging an office may seem like a minor change, to you this is a total shake up of your normal routine! You're not just going to go in the next day and be totally comfortable in your new surroundings. There is going to be some pain, some adjustment, and some compromise that has to take place in order to make things work.

But after a week, two weeks, or maybe even a month, things will begin to feel normal, and you will have an expected routine again. This same scenario applies to your kids.

We are all human beings in this life together. Give yourself and your kids time to adjust, but don't give up trying. I think most parents would agree that your children are the most important investment in life so why so often do we seem to avoid investing more deeply into them?

2. Control Your Reactions.

Asking and then truly listening can be a challenge at times; but, as parents, controlling our reactions to what our children tell us can be just as hard. For parents (moms especially), listening to our daughters' struggles can bring up a lot of memories from our own past.

Many memories may be painful ones. Just the other day, my preschool daughter said that two of her friends told her she couldn't play with them that day. She just couldn't understand why they wouldn't want to play with her. Before she had even finished her story, my mind jumped back to the merry-go-round when I was in kindergarten. I remember pushing it all by myself and then trying to hop on without falling. I wished that someone would come play and take turns pushing. No one ever came. Such a small part of my life but that same sad, lonely feeling I had that day on the merry-go-round came right back and hit me like a ton of bricks at that moment. My heart broke thinking that Tinley may have to experience those same feelings of loneliness that I did. At the same time another part of my brain was already forming a very distinct plan on how to handle this situation.

As a mom we want to fix things (which we will talk about later) and at that moment I had a very distinct solution. The plan was to wait till I saw the girls walking into school the next day, stop them in their tracks, proceed to ask them what in the world was their problem, what made them so special that they could tell Tinley she couldn't play with them? Then I would tell them the answer. NOTHING! Then I'd go on to tell them how special Tin was and how it was their loss and that they better watch who they are mean to next time. Then I would make a bee-line for the parents and inform them of their daughters' abhorrent behavior toward my precious, innocent, little girl, aaannnddd... Yeah, I should probably stop myself here. I realize this is probably not the best way to go about handling the situation, but in that moment those thoughts were the first to pop into my head. Thankfully, I took a deep breath before I spoke, gathered my thoughts, and tried to separate my impulse feelings from rational ones.

"Tin, I'm so sorry to hear that. Did that make you feel sad?"

"Yeah."

"You know what, Tin, if that happens again, it's okay to tell them that acting that way isn't nice. If they still don't want to play with you, then you can just tell them it's their loss and find someone who is nice to play with."

Although this might not have been the proper textbook response, it did get a basic life principle across to her in a way that was composed and rational. I wanted her to know that it's okay to address a person when they aren't treating you properly. It is also important to let yourself, as well as others, know that you are of value. I wanted her to know that she didn't need to surround herself with people who were going to make her feel sad. Instead, she needs to learn to transform her surroundings into a place where she feels happy and accepted.

These are all basic life principles that I want her to take with her and use—not just throughout her school days, but throughout her life. Why not have her start using these tools now when she's young so she knows how to handle situations when she becomes an adult?

I was so proud of Tinley a few days later when I asked,

"Hey, babe, how was school? Did you play with anyone exciting today?"

"Yeah, I played with _____ and _____."

"Oh, really? Were they nice to you today?"

"Yup! I went up and asked them if I could play with them and told them, 'Please don't tell me 'no' like last time because that isn't very nice!'"

She went on to say how they seemed surprised and said they didn't remember saying that. Pretty soon they were as happy as could be playing together again. Oh, if only all women's drama were solved that easily!

3. Stop Interrupting.

We reprimand our children for interrupting when they are young, so it's ironic that some of the very things we punish our children for are the things we end up doing to them! Interrupting when our children are trying to tell us something seems to be a big issue parents struggle with. It is so important to listen to the whole story before jumping in with our input! (As many of you parents already know, the story your child is telling you could change five times from beginning to end!) During the first half of the story, you may be thinking about taking your child out of that "awful, no good" school and homeschooling from now on, just to realize by the end of the story that as much as you may want to deny it, it was actually your child causing the issue in the first place.

I understand that every story is different and every child is different, but allowing them to speak without interrupting and keeping an objective mind (to whatever extent you can as a parent) does wonders for your relationship with your children. Sometimes they don't want to hear your opinion on a subject; they just want you to listen. Talking together can be a simple, yet somehow very difficult, task. Your children's desire to share their thoughts with you is a good indicator that they trust you. Don't eliminate that trust by opening your mouth too soon or being distracted by something else going on!

My mom didn't always have an answer for me when I was upset about something. Sometimes all she could do was hold me while I cried and stay with me until I settled down. A lot of times that is all I needed. Other times, she would give me her perspective on the situation, but she always allowed me to express my feelings whether she agreed with me or not. One thing she never did was tell me she didn't have time to hear what I was saying or leave in the middle of my sharing something with her.

4. You Don't Have to "Fix It"

As moms, our job is to fix things. The baby's hungry? We feed him. The Barbie doll lost an arm again? We glue it back on. The dog pooped in the house for the third time this week? We clean it up… again.

We fix things every day, all day without even thinking about it. It's second nature to us, and we do a very good job at it. So when it comes to our children, it can be hard to not just "fix" their problems for them. After all, we can see the whole picture while they are only seeing a small part, right? They don't have the knowledge, understanding, or life experience as we do so why not make it easy on everyone and just take control of the situation and fix it? That's our mentality a lot of times, isn't it?

Well, hold on to your yoga pants, mamas! Have you ever thought that maybe—just maybe—you don't have all the answers? That maybe your children need to make their own mistakes (to an extent) in order to grow and learn?

Or...here's a thought that's really "out there." I hesitate to even say it, but maybe your children have some really good thoughts and opinions of their own that might not be the same as yours. (This is largely due to your awesome parental guidance in showing them the importance of forming their own opinions throughout the years!)

Step back in time for a minute and think about some of the best lessons you've learned in life. Did the lessons come from watching your parents fix a mess you had created? Or were they lessons you learned from cleaning up the mess yourself?

While it is our job as parents to keep our child healthy and safe, it is also our job to let them grow, discover their own unique personalities, and learn things for themselves in order to prepare them for when they leave home. Finding a good balance of when/where to allow them to make mistakes can be tough, and I don't think any parent has it mastered. I know I don't! However, by continuing to ask the question, "Would this be a good learning experience for my child?" may help guide us in determining when to step in and when to let go.

5. Moving On & Letting Go.

While interviewing women for this project it became very apparent that one of the biggest issues facing both parents and teens in their relationship is the ability to communicate openly and honestly with each other. Parents get frustrated that their child won't share more with them and yet the child gets frustrated because of the parents' subjectivity and bias toward their child that sometimes deters them from wanting to talk about things. When I asked the question, "Do you talk to your parents about struggles you are having with friends?" many responded similarly to this woman, "Talked to Mom sometimes, but it was hard because if she knew someone hurt me, then a month later I became friends with the person who hurt me, she still had that perception of the girl from a month ago. I hid a lot from my parents. Looking back, I wish my mom wouldn't have always sided with me. She didn't help me remove myself from the situation and see my part in it."

When people hurt those we love, we can automatically put them in the "villain" category of our brains. Even after a situation has been resolved, because we haven't been included in the resolution and are not seeing firsthand how it was handled, we hold on to those negative past feelings about those who hurt our loved one.

Having experienced this several times myself, I tend to pour my heart out to those I love and trust when someone/something upsets me. Most of the time, a couple days later the issue gets resolved and is usually the result of a miscommunication. I move on, and life is good again; however, the next time that person comes up in conversation, I realize those I shared my experience with still have the same bias and subjectivity (and rightfully so) that I had during the heat of the moment of conflict. The conflict has not been resolved in their minds, due in part to my not telling them the way the issue had been resolved. This is a common mistake people make, and I have been trying to make a conscious effort when I tell someone something in an emotional state to make sure I also share with them when the issue is resolved. That way I can put their minds at ease, as well as my own.

Although it can be hard to understand why your daughter is making certain choices when it comes to relationships, it's important not to overly involve your own emotions in her relationships. If there is a conflict, it's more than likely that your child will figure out how to re-solve it. There are only so many times that we (and our children!) can stick our fingers in the fire before realizing it hurts and move away from the heat. Some people figure it out the first time, but others have to get burned a few times before backing away.

Try to look at any situation from an objective perspective. I am aware this can be difficult, especially when you're only hearing one side. It's important to focus on the whole picture instead of just the side that you are hearing. If you do this, you will be better equipped to guide your child in a direction they may not have thought about be-fore. And through your objective advice, they will be better equipped to make a more rational, informed decision about how to deal with conflict.

However, at the same time, we also have to remember that our children are still growing and learning how to find their way. They may not always make the right decision in your eyes, and in some instances, that is okay. The best thing you may be able to do for them during this time is remind them of the values and principles with which they have been raised. Then, as my mom would say, you pray.

Pray every day, sometimes every hour. No matter how much we would like to be that fly on the wall everywhere our child is, we cannot be with them all the time. This is where you have to trust the child you raised and pray that God will guide their decisions. And for the times they don't make the right decisions, you show grace while also enforcing the principles and rules you have set. Let them know that you are disappointed in the choice that was made and remind them that they will have to face consequences for the action they chose. But then also let them know that your love for them will nev-er change and extend a certain amount of grace during these tough times. Doing this shows that, no matter what, you will always be there for them and that they can count on you to love them through any and all situations.

Let me be clear: I am NOT encouraging you to allow your children to make any choice they want and support them in it. We obviously need to use common sense as parents, and I totally support parents when they need to step in and prevent a situation that could be detrimental to their children's well-being.

One parent I interviewed put it well: "Potentially allowing our children to make mistakes ensures that they know that we will be there no matter what. I don't want to be a friend, but I still want to be the mom that other girls feel comfortable talking to. But I should always be thought of as a mom. They need to know there is a line of authority there."

There can be a very fine line between protecting our children and over-stepping our bounds. However, in general, allowing our children to choose their own path is part of successful parenting.

I would like to end this chapter with a saying I've heard for years and years: "If someone isn't getting the attention they need at home, they will look elsewhere for it." This goes for anyone—your spouse, your child; heck, even your dog will go away if it's not being cared for and nurtured! And although those seeking attention may not realize it, many of the places they look are not always the healthiest. However, because they are desperate for the feelings of love and affection, they may settle for an artificial substitute or instant gratification to fill that void, even though in the end, it will only make that void bigger. Think about that the next time you decide to take a call instead of listening to your child. It might help you put things into a little better perspective.

CHAPTER **13**

Straight from the Experts

IN MY EXPERIENCE you can read as many parenting books as you want, research statistics, and peruse scholarly journals about adolescent behavior and how to best handle situations, yet you may still face a world of unknowns when it comes to raising children. Or you can go straight to the people who have put in the work, done the time and raised successful human beings. You can talk to them about how they did it.

Although I have done my share of scholarly research, and some of it was very helpful, in my opinion I'd much rather learn from someone who has had hands-on experience. Because of this, I wanted to discover what I call "super awesome mamas" and get some advice from them about how to raise "super awesome kids." Here are some of words of wisdom that stuck out to me as learned from these women and reflected on my own parenting and what type of parent I want to be.

1. *"I'm involved. I attend things at their school. I'm a room parent. I'm at all the PIT (parent involvement team) crew events. I can see my daughter from a different perspective this way. Being involved is huge." ~Mother of school age children*

I have begun to notice how important this is in my own life with my daughter. Although I never in my wildest dreams pictured myself as the "room mom," I find myself this year becoming exactly that! I volunteer occasionally in Tinley's class to help out. I did this originally because she was missing me during the day, and I was trying to think of ways I could make her days a little easier. As I volunteer, I find that I see a different side of Tinley that I don't necessarily get to see at home. I see how she interacts with other kids and how other kids perceive her. I get to see what types of friends she is choosing, and I'm also getting to see what a cool human being she really is becoming.

I also find that getting to know the parents can be very beneficial. Tinley's preschool class only had about fifteen kids, so every day I could see the same parents, grandparents, and babysitters take and drop off the kids at school. There were many days we would stay after school and let the kids play on the playground for a few minutes. As this happened, I naturally began to interact with the parents. I was able to form friendly relationships with many of the moms and form a "bond" with them that remains as our children have started elementary school. Although our children are not all in the same class anymore, we still have a sense of "watching out" for each other's little ones because of the bond we formed over the previous couple of years.

One of the parents recently went to school to have lunch with her son and told me she saw Tinley looking sad. This mom went up and asked if Tin was okay when she noticed that Tinley was sitting by two rowdy boys who were "razzing" her. This mom went up to those boys and told them to knock it off and be nice to Tin. She told them she saw exactly what was going on!

I had to laugh when I heard this. These are the types of parents that are good to have in your corner! And while I don't want to be the mom who picks out their kids' friends, I don't necessarily think it's bad to direct your children toward types of kids who you feel would be healthy for them. You are the parent. You are the protector. Would you go for a walk and see a snake in your child's direct path without telling her to watch out? It's called being a good parent.

As your kids get older, this gets even more important. They are going to want to have sleepovers and go to each other's houses for birthday parties, etc. Call me an overly protective parent, but I am NOT going to allow my child to go into someone's home if I'm not 100% comfortable with it. In today's society, you can't be too cautious. It's just too easy for something to happen.

I understand we cannot be 100% all-knowing, but we can definitely be smart about things! Get to know the families of your child's friends, ask others about them, see how they interact with their children, get to know the parents yourself. Heck, call me crazy, but do a criminal background check if you need to before letting your child into their home!

Coming from a small town, I'm aware that I may have an advantage in this area because everyone seems to know everyone, and it's probably easier to pick out the good apples from the bad, but you can never be too sure. Our job is to be the parent, the protector, not the friend. Right now, Tinley has about three or four friends. I feel totally comfortable with letting her go to their houses without my presence, and every one of them is either a parent I am friends with or someone I have known for a lengthy amount of time and have been around to see their parenting and home life in action. These are the only homes I will allow my daughter to go into without me. She can love me or hate me for that, but I'm not willing to take any chances.

2. *"The world doesn't revolve around your child being the most popular. What matters is that you raise a caring, considerate child. It's hard to watch your child hurt, but don't let yourself get too wrapped up in it. It will get better. I always talked to my kids like they were adults. They knew they could talk to me about anything. Looking back as a parent, I would say to other parents, keep things in perspective. It's not the end of the world. Also try not to let yourself be as hurt as they are about things."~Mother of adult children*

Do you remember the scene in the movie *Mean Girls* where the mom of one of the "plastics" (plastics refers to the small, elite group of popular girls)" comes into the room dressed like a teenager? She tries to act like she is one of them and brings them "cocktails" to drink. I think she even says something like, "I'm not like the other moms. I'm a cool mom." She lets her daughter treat her like dirt and does whatever her daughter wants. Regina (the daughter) ends up having a lot of stuff go wrong for her. However, the mom is so worried about her and her daughter being popular that she takes a back seat to being a parent.

Have you seen this in real life? I definitely have in my own school experience and even now looking at some of the moms around the area . They want so much for their child to be accepted that they allow things to go on that most responsible parents would say "no way" to!

It may be because of their own teenage experiences and a powerful desire to find acceptance now from their children and their children's friends. Perhaps subconsciously a mother may even try to seek acceptance from these kids in order to make up for a lack of acceptance from her peers when she was younger. But no matter the reason, the end result is usually for the parent the same. The child becomes the boss, and the parent becomes the child. The end result for the child is irresponsibility, disrespect, and unpreparedness for what the real world is going to bring to them in just a few short years.

Popularity isn't going to last very long if you are not a decent human being. You can only "fake it" for so long before people catch on to your game. Wouldn't you rather teach your children how to respect people, work hard, and earn what they get? Those qualities are going to bring your child so much more success in life than making sure they have the right clothes or get into the right parties as teenagers.

And think about this--what happens in a few short years when your children are gone and off on their own? What will you be left thinking about yourself?

I see these moms and even some students who have graduated

come back the next year to the sporting events or concerts still thinking they are "big stuff" only to find that the next year's "court" has taken their spot and they are really just "the leftovers." There you are—left out and forgotten. Kind of stinks, huh?

Teach your children what is important and what is fleeting in life. It will get them much farther in life than a little popularity will get them now.

3. *"Pray for your children when you lie down, when you get up, when you go through your day." ~mother of adult children*

Personally, being a woman of faith I don't think you can pray too much for your child. There is a lot we can do to help guide and protect our children but there are some things that are out of our hands. That is when we have to put our faith in a higher power and trust that God's will be done. Knowing when I was in school that my mom was praying for me throughout the day and sometimes at specific times during the day often helped and gave me a sense of peace.

4. *"Find a support system. If you don't have close friends who you can trust and share with, then find an organization near you. Two excellent ones are Moms in Touch and Mothers of Preschoolers (MOPS). Also joining a small group or Bible study is beneficial. Get involved with a local church that will support both you and your children." ~mother of adult children*

Like I mentioned previously, I have gone to a mom's group for about three years now and it has been a tremendous blessing! It's so refreshing to connect with other moms. Even if you're not talking specifically about your children it's constructive just to have a group of women in the same life-stage who can relate to some of what you are going through. This can be so beneficial to your mind, body, and soul.

5. *"If you are married, take time for each other. Every night we would sit on the porch or at the dinner table and just talk. Nourish your marriage. Spend time together. Let your kids see what a husband and wife relationship should look like. They are watching, and it will help them more than anything when they start to date to know what a healthy relationship should look like."*

This piece of advice is from my mom, and it is really true. I remember my parents talking to each other almost every night after dinner or going out and sitting on the front porch together. I didn't realize what an impact this had on me until I got married. I suddenly started forming the same habits they had without even realizing it. Now with two kids and another on the way, it's so important for both my husband and me to have "our time." We try to have a date night once a week where it's just us without the kids. We have time to connect and talk about what's been going on in our lives. As parents, we need time to reconnect with our spouse. I remembering hearing this a long time ago, and it has stayed with me: "Your children are lent to you for eighteen years, but your spouse is with you for a lifetime." Invest in your relationship now so, once your children are gone, your marriage isn't gone as well.

6. *"During teenage years when peer pressure to do things that kids shouldn't be doing becomes almost unbearable, give your kids a reason not to do it. Do this so they can tell their friends why they can't do something. Provide an escape for them from the temptation. Set the rules for your kids before the temptation comes, and tell them what the consequences will be. For example, I told my girls that if they were ever caught drinking, they would not have a car for a year. I didn't tell them that because I wanted to be a hard-nosed mom; I did it to give them a reason to say no. The punishment was so severe that when they told their*

friends, even the friends wouldn't pressure them because it was so hard. "mother of adult children

Don't be afraid to be the 'bad guy.' Who cares if your kid's friends think you are a jerk. If it means my kids have a way out of a bad situation at my expense it's totally worth it!

7. *"If your child has a goal or dream, don't crush it. Let your children know you believe in them and that you will help them achieve that goal if at all possible. Tabitha wanted to make the volleyball team in the 8th grade so we went outside and played volleyball almost every night. We talked to her older cousin who had played and we asked her to give lessons. We attended a volleyball camp together that was offered by our church, and we learned together. Amazingly, Tabitha made the volleyball team. In high school, she decided she wanted to be a cheerleader. Again, we did what we could to help her succeed. We even turned our living room into a gymnasium by moving all the furniture to make a big open space so she could learn to do cartwheels! Again, she made the team. Although our kids didn't always succeed at everything they wanted to do, they knew they had our support and that we would come right alongside them to help them accomplish those goals and dreams. I truly believe that actions do speak louder than words."*

Again, words spoken by my mom are so true! One of the funniest and most embarrassing memories of my teenage years was practicing for cheerleading tryouts in my living room. I will be the first to admit, I probably should not have made the squad. I am about as uncoordinated as they come—a gymnastics dropout—and it took me a long time before I could master a basic cartwheel.

My parents supported me, though. My dad even did a few

cartwheels to show me how to do them. (I think his cartwheels were better than my own—not that that's saying too much!)

Did they possibly think I didn't have a chance at making it? If I were them, I would have thought so, but they never let on it if they did. They only gave me affirmation and encouragement. And when by some miracle, I made the team, they were just as excited as I was. Which leads to our last piece of advice…

8. *"Don't be afraid to affirm your kids. When they are at school, it's possible that their spirits are being crushed daily; kids can be very self-centered and will do whatever it takes to bring other kids down in order to bring themselves up. Tell your kids every day that you love them. Don't be afraid to tell them how special they are. Help to build up their self-esteem because all around them it is being crushed." "Speak truth to them even if it's hard. Mold them into the persons God wants them to be." ~mother of adult children*

Almost every morning when I was growing up, my mom would wake me up by singing the same songs. Although seriously annoying at the moment, it turned out to be a fond memory I cherish as an adult. One of the songs, I think she made up goes like this, "Who's the prettiest, who's the prettiest, prettiest little girl in the town…." That was my cue to chime in and say, "ME!" which at 7:00 a.m. in the morning I rarely did. But even just a silly song like that, sung repeatedly, I think subconsciously built up my confidence.

I've heard before that it takes ten compliments to erase one insult. I would agree with this statement. If someone grants me a compliment I seem to usually brush it off and sometimes almost feel guilty for accepting it. However if someone insults me, it eats away at my core for hours if not days if I let it. So although we don't want our children to become conceited and think of themselves as better than others, it is important that they hear from their parents how special they truly are. It helps build both character and confidence.

CHAPTER 14

Final Thoughts

GROWING UP IS tough. Being a parent is tough. Everyone handles their struggles differently and relies on different skills to help them navigate through their struggles in life.

Looking back on my teenage years I now see how I could have handled some of my friendships differently and would have possibly had some different outcomes in certain relationships had I known then what I know now; however, I am also grateful for the experiences because they shaped me into the person I am today.

Looking toward the future there are a couple of things I would like to leave you with that I hope may help anyone—no matter what age— when struggling to find meaning and value in relationships.

1. Be Aware of Your Own Intentions When Forming a Relationship.

You know when your intentions are good and when they are not. There is only so long a person can disguise artificial happiness for the real thing. Even when you think you are coming across as genuine, if within yourself your motives are otherwise, that will quickly shine through. People are attracted to those who lift them up, who encourage them, who help them become better people. These are all qualities of a good friend. Something to ask yourself or your child when forming a new relationship: "What are my intentions for this relationship? Are my motives sincere and honest? If the answer is no you need to seriously re-evaluate your pursuit of the relationship. If the origin is insincere it is more than likely based on deceit and selfishness, which is not beneficial to either party involved, and will eventually lead to struggles and conflict. Not every relationship you have will succeed, even if you have good intentions, but I can assure you of one thing: if you are not genuine, your relationship will not be fulfilling and probably won't last.

2. Confidence Is Key.

Being confident that you are worth a good relationship is crucial. If you don't think you are worth it, then who else will? This again starts with being genuine and sincere with yourself first and then with the person with whom you are involved. As women we are blessed with the gift of intuition. We can sense things and understand things that may not be outwardly seen or heard. By combining our logic, our intuition, and our heart, we can many times discern if a relationship is worth pursuing or not. If we evaluate it and realize a relationship is not healthy, being confident enough in ourselves to allow that relationship to end can be a valuable asset and save a lot of stress in the future.

It's also worth noting the seasons of relationships (specifically speaking of friendships) and realizing the value of each type. Some friends will be with you for one season of your life, while others will be with you for a lifetime. Both types of friends are important to have. God knows what you need at different times in your life. Just because a friend that you had in high school isn't your friend in college doesn't mean the relationship was worthless. You learn things about yourself and others through your relationships. Sometimes there isn't any real reason it ended. You may have just lost touch or gone your separate ways, and that is okay.

Try to embrace relationships for what they are and accept where they go. Focus on what you learned about yourself through the relationship. For example, what types of qualities did I appreciate in this person and what traits in a friend do I want to stay away from in the future? Did I feel good around this person, and if not, why?

Asking questions like these—and even writing them down in some cases—can help you better know what to look for in future relationships. Relationships, whether seasonal or FFL (friends for life), are great learning experiences. I once heard that if on your deathbed you can say you have one good friend, you are a very blessed person. I would agree.

Conclusion

THIS BOOK HAS been a healing journey for me, and I thank you for allowing me to pour out some of my heart to you. I would encourage all of you to take some time to evaluate your own life—past, present, and future. Allow yourself to be real with who you were in your past, who you are now, and who you want to be in your future. Our experiences—both good and bad—shape us into who we are today.

God has created us to be perfectly imperfect! Use your experiences to help others who may be going through the same things. God has a plan for you. He allows us to go through trials and hardships for a reason, to help shape us into the people he created us to be. Don't let your purpose go to waste by hiding behind a veil of shame or pain. Love it! Embrace the perfectly imperfect woman God created you to be!

Works Cited

"Bully, Bullied, Bullying, Social isolation." *Dictionary.com*. Dictionary, 2017. Web. 19 November 2017.

Lally, P.,van Jaarsveld, C.H.M.,Potts, H.W.W. and Wardle, J. "How are habits formed: Modelling habit formation in the real world." http://onlinelibrary.wiley.com/doi/10./1002/ejsp.674/full.   John Wiley & Sons, Ltd,16 July 2009.

Mean Girls. Dir. Mark Waters. Perf. Lindsay Lohan, Jonathan Bennett, Rachel McAdams. Paramount Pictures, 2004. DVD.

The Bible. NIV Study Bible, Grand Rapids, Mi, 2002.

William Shakespeare. Quote: *"A friend is one who knows who you are, understands where you have been, accepts what you have become and still gently allows you to grow."* English Dramatist, Playwright, Poet. 1564-1616.

CPSIA information can be obtained
at www.ICGtesting.com
Printed in the USA
LVHW04s2058100918
589678LV00002B/21/P